Soul Fingers

The Music & Life of Legendary Bassist

Donald "Duck" Dunn

By Nick Rosaci

To professional musicians everywhere

PLAYBACK+
Speed • Pitch • Balance • Loop

To access audio visit:
www.halleonard.com/mylibrary

Enter Code
4416-7796-4504-7220

Cover photo courtesy of Dunn Family Archives

ISBN 978-1-4950-5292-7

7777 W. BLUEMOUND RD. P.O. BOX 13819 MILWAUKEE, WI 53213

Visit Hal Leonard Online at
www.halleonard.com

Contents

Foreword
by Dan Aykroyd

First and foremost, there would have been no credible Blues Brothers record, touring act, or legitimate success had Donald "Duck" Dunn not been our bass player. His collaboration and friendship with 19-year-old drummer Steve Jordan drove our music as no backbone percussive duo could have. Moreover, as John Belushi and I assembled the band with Paul Shaffer and Tom Malone, the signing of Duck and Steve Cropper—who were the core of Stax-Volt—immediately underwrote the Blues Brothers band as the genuine article.

The first Blues Brothers record, *Briefcase Full of Blues*, went triple platinum with over 3.5 million recorded units sold—a number which top artists today would be immensely pleased with. A success of this degree would never have occurred were it not specifically for Duck's counsel. To John and I, he said:

"Sure, the blues is great, and sure, right now we've got the super blues band of the century, but if we only cut blues tracks and release them, Blues Brothers or not, you won't sell a million records—not with only blues cuts. Right now the music industry and the world are experiencing a temporary gap in popular music. The disco era has just ended and this new punk/new wave movement that John likes has not caught fire yet. But if we cut 'Soul Man' and put it on the record as the lead track, I guarantee you a million-seller."

How right Duck was! Not only did he usher us to a #1 charting hit with our cover of "Soul Man," but Duck's extensive and highly eclectic knowledge of American music opened up vast choices of superb material from the Stax-Volt catalog and other sources of sometimes obscure songs. Duck turned us onto Wynonie Harris and Lowell Fulson, artists whose songs I still sing today when the privilege presents itself.

Beyond the above, Duck provided a massive stabilizing force among the sometimes fractious relationships which can evolve in musical cohesions. Duck was a peacemaker even when he was fighting with Al Rubin about something. He was fiery and passionate but also humble and self-effacing.

Duck was tough but really sweet, and by far the funniest member of the band. *The Blues Brothers* film captured some of his essence, but on the road, he was a continuous source of humor—ironic views of everyone and everything, with healthy doses of anarchy. In the end, all were impressed with his qualities as a magnetic human being, his abilities as a master craftsman, and his professionalism as a team member. To declare Donald "Duck" Dunn as a beloved figure, in the perspective of industry personnel and his friends, would not be debated by those who had the pleasure and privilege of knowing and working with him.

The power and penetration of his music around the world and in history cannot be overstated. It was his bass lines on "Ninety-Nine and a Half" and several other tunes at the time that thrummed deep in the American hooches of Vietnam, giving thousands of dutiful service men and women comfort throughout that war.

During the struggle for civil rights in the 1960s, Stax-Volt was an integrated recording house. Duck stood on the right side of the issue through his embrace and support of the African-American artists who defined that generation of music built on traditional blues and R&B, which produced a unique appeal in popular culture.

If Duck were still with us, he would still be playing, performing, and recording, and in the process, thrilling audiences live as he did until the night he passed through the veil.

His legacy and contribution to our lives will be with us forever.

—*Dan Aykroyd,
a.k.a. Elwood Blues*

Courtesy Photofest

Introduction

I was a jazz bass student in college and excited to be on my first (of what would be many) of what I like to call "mansion gigs." As the name implies, it was a jazz trio gig at a mansion in a sub-development on a golf course, and I had to drive through a security guardhouse and explain where I was going.

An elderly man opened up the door, and his eyes lit up when he saw my upright bass in the bed of my truck. This man told me that his favorite bass player was a guy by the name of Donald "Duck" Dunn. I politely acted interested as he told me he was the bass player in *The Blues Brothers* movie. I loved the movie, so I was a little more interested, but thought that a blues bass player was beneath me, especially with the CDs of players like Victor Wooten and Jaco Pastorius in my truck. Over time, I did pay a little more attention to the bass player in the movie and his two short but funny lines, his pipe, and his collection of Fender Precision basses.

On lots of different gigs in my 20s, I would get dirty looks from the bandleaders, telling me to either "play the ink," or that I played "way too many notes." I always went home and scoffed at the feedback, thinking I was just doing the same thing that the bass greats were doing, and that the bandleader wouldn't care what those guys were playing if they were on the stage. It wasn't until my late 20s that an older musician took me off to the side and asked me if I'd ever checked out this bass player by the name of Duck Dunn. I told him, "Sure, I've heard of him, but I haven't really studied his bass lines." By this point, I'd studied James Jamerson and his style and thought that was what a bass player should do on a tune he doesn't know—bounce around and play some fills. But while doing this, I was never really locking in with the drummer.

One afternoon, I was watching *The Blues Brothers* movie (for probably the millionth time) and decided to learn Duck's line from "Sweet Home Chicago." Duck would say that he's not a jazz musician, but now that I've seen this movie so many times, I'd pit that walking bass line against Paul Chambers or Ray Brown. He's not walking over "Giant Steps" or a line of ii-V-I's, but that pocket was unparalleled.

Doing an internet search, I found a disappointingly small amount of transcriptions available. There was an out-of-print book fetching outlandish prices on the used market. There were a few transcriptions here and there, mostly

from his Stax work, but no "Sweet Home Chicago." I found that Duck had played with some great musicians outside of Stax, but there was very little information on that as well. Being a music copyist and offering transcription services on the side, I decided to write my own book.

Throughout my research, I have been contacted by many musicians and technicians who have told me how happy they are that this book is being done. "If anybody deserves this, it's Duck," more than one have said.

While researching, it became evident that Duck was more than an influential bass player. In a personal sense, he left an imprint on many people's lives. His bad jokes and goofy delivery still induce raucous laughter, sometimes just because the person is remembering Duck's laughter while trying to finish the joke. It was obvious that Duck left joy with people wherever he went and sincerely cared about everyone. "I think that you will find out that everybody loved Duck, number one," were the first words out of Steve Cropper's mouth when he spoke to me. "What you will find out about Duck Dunn is that it was more about Duck the *character* than it was Duck the *bass player*."

Dunn Family Archives

Photo by Marco Rabatti/James R. Taylor

The date this book was expected to be finished was pushed back a number of times because so many people wanted to speak their mind about Duck. And the enthusiasm that came with each of those phone calls showed they sincerely loved Duck and wanted this book to be the best that it could be. One of the most pleasant aspects of working on it was sharing laughs with the people who helped shape American popular music. Of course, recording the accompanying audio tracks was another highlight of the journey.

Throughout the book, I used many quotes from Duck's friends, family, and colleagues; the facts are somewhere within them, but not always immediately apparent. Some of these stories are 50, 60, or 70 years old, and to the witnesses of these stories, it obviously wasn't something they thought they'd be telling someone so far into the future.

This book is more than a transcription book. It's a glimpse into the life of one musician and the impact he has made on popular music as a whole—not simply in one studio for roughly 15 years, but around the world with a career

of over five decades. The book attempts to dissect Duck's style and what made him so unique. It's also meant to teach younger bassists that playing more notes doesn't always equate to a better bass line. The feel is more important than how many notes you can shred over one chord in a measure. It's a testament to the relationship between bassist and drummer (or bassist and guitarist)—it is more than just a friendship; it's a rapport that the success of the song depends on.

So pull up a chair and enjoy Duck's story with a hot dish of fatback cacciatore or an aromatic pipe tobacco, with the sounds of his bass accompanying Otis or the Blues Brothers playing in the background.

—Nick Rosaci

Chapter 1:
Southern Roots

With so few people left to talk about Duck's early life, his older brother, Charley Dunn, was more than happy to reminisce. I asked few questions and mainly let Charley just talk about his experiences with Duck. As other friends and family members joined the ranks to share their experiences, it slowly became a full story pieced together like a puzzle, where each piece made more sense as they all joined together, painting a fuller picture.

Despite the stereotype of the musician leading a party lifestyle, carelessly partaking in habits that would ultimately lead to an untimely death, Duck led a life that someone might call fulfilled. If there was an ideal bassist, Duck would be it: charming, witty, full of life, and no ego to boot. Don Nix, one of Duck's best friends and a colleague throughout his life, summed it up perfectly: "I can't conceive growing up without Duck Dunn. He made it fun. Whenever he was around, he made everybody feel good. He don't hold grudges or anything and never argued. He was just a happy guy."

Duckling (Dunn Family Archives)

Duck was born November 24, 1941, at St. Joseph's Hospital in Memphis, Tennessee, as the sixth of seven children. Coincidentally, Wayne Jackson, would-be trumpet player with the Mar-Keys, was born in the same hospital on the

same day. Not only was Duck born in the south, like most R&B musicians, but in Memphis—an historic musical hodgepodge of more than a few American-born genres. His father, James Blaine, worked as a candy maker, and his mother, Nana Belle, was a homemaker. Having a name closely resembling the Disney character Donald Duck, his father gave him the nickname that would stick for the rest of his life. "Dad gave us all nicknames right away; I even got the nickname 'Stinky' because I once had a real stinky diaper!" Duck's brother, Charley, said through a small chuckle.

Duck's love of music was instilled early on and nurtured throughout his childhood. According to Charley, Duck could pull any record you asked for off the shelf before he could even walk. "You'd tell Duck which record you wanted, and he would crawl over to the shelf, pull it out, and bring it over to you."

Around the age of two, Duck got a hold of some matches and lit the gas on the stove. The ensuing accident caused him to be in and out of the hospital for the better part of the next year. He was left with scar tissue that limited the movement of his left arm. Having been born left handed, this made many simple tasks difficult, as he had to learn how to do them with his right hand instead. The scarring left Duck self-conscious about taking off his shirt, and he rarely did so. In an interview in 2009, Duck said, "I got burnt pretty bad. And so I was laid up until the time I was about the first grade. But my brother, we used to listen to the Grand Ole Opry… but then when I heard Little Richard and Bill Doggett and Bo Diddley, of course, it just changed my life."

Music wasn't the only skill Duck would learn. At the age of nine, Duck got a yoyo and practiced it seemingly around the clock. Three years later, Duck came in second place in a yoyo competition at Overton Park in 1954. Duck would continue to bring his yoyo with him and play with it during downtime, including while on tour. "Duck was real good with his hands and could do anything with them," Charley said. It was obvious he was proud of his brother. At ten, Duck was given a ukulele and played it whenever he was able to. He just never wanted to stop playing.

It was in sixth grade that Duck was transferred to a new school and met his lifelong friends: Don Nix, who would

*Duck, 12, with yoyo champion James Hamilton, 15
(Dunn Family Archives)*

play saxophone with the Mar-Keys, and Steve Cropper, who would work with Duck in the Mar-Keys, Booker T. & the MGs, and later on with the Blues Brothers. Steve Cropper remembers the first time he met Duck: "What I do remember, I don't think we thought anything funny that his name was Duck. But he did tell me that his dad named him that after Donald Duck the cartoon character. But Duck had red hair, and a big spot right in the top middle about a half an inch back, and it was a different color. It looked like somebody had dropped some paint, and it was a different color than the rest of it."

At first, the friends were a typical American group of boys. They followed sports and played outside together. If football was in season, they would get together and play. If baseball or basketball was in season, they'd do the same thing. Don and Duck's mothers were best friends, and Cropper lived in the same neighborhood, so the three saw lots of each other.

Well before they played any instruments, Duck, Steve, and Don rode the bus downtown every Saturday. They enjoyed visiting Lansky Brothers Clothing Store on Beale Street. The business was famous for cloth-

Dunn Family Archives

ing many famous musicians, including Elvis Presley and B.B. King, and would go on to dress Isaac Hayes and Eddie Floyd. Elvis was quickly rising in popularity, and the boys wanted to dress the part. So why not shop where the future "King" shops?

It wasn't until around tenth grade that the boys started taking up music. In the '50s, Memphis was rich with some of the most famous names in music: Bobby Bland, Memphis Slim, Johnny Ace, Muddy Waters, Johnny Cash, B.B. King, Jerry Lee Lewis, Elvis Presley, the list goes on and on. So, it was inevitable that this musical city would cultivate the next generation of musicians. And with these boys, it did just that. They occasionally headed out to the night clubs and attempted to sneak in—sometimes successfully and sometimes not. One of their favorite places was Plantation Inn, where they would eventually meet future Stax members, along with Ben Branch. Branch was a popular bandleader in the Memphis area and would be a source of influence for these young musicians.

Duck's performance in school started to decline and grades were dropping. Instead of doing homework, he was spending his time listening to music or looking in the mirror, trying to copy the movements of Elvis Presley or Frankie Lymon. Duck and Steve, along with their friend Charlie Freeman and occasionally other neighborhood kids, regularly got together to learn guitar. During school, they spent time in the smoking room, smoking cigarettes and learning to play their instruments. According to Steve, "Duck wanted to play. Well, he couldn't quite grasp the guitar. But since a kid, which I didn't know, he'd been playing a little ukulele and all, which has four strings. One day, he shows up at rehearsal with a bass."

After speaking with several sources, the details of Duck's first bass were difficult to pin down. The first one was likely a Kay K-162 Electronic Bass. Not only did a bass seem to be a better fit for Duck, but it filled a need for him and his friends. Better yet, it had four strings, much like the ukulele he used to play. His first bass was bought from Larry Brown, the house bassist at the Plantation Inn. Brown taught Duck his first few lessons to get him started, and Duck credits Brown for the basis of his feel.

Duck learned to play bass mainly by listening to records and the radio. Much of the musical influence on the boys came from a Memphis DJ by the name of Dewey Phillips and his radio show "Red, Hot, and Blue." The show was well-known for being "out of the box," as Phillips would do things like play the same song over and over the whole day, just because he liked it. Phillips played, among other things, what were known as "race records"—music of black musicians at the time largely ignored by most radio stations and very hard to find. The shows were an eclectic mixture of current music, ranging from soul to country to jazz to big band, and everything in between.

Eventually, Duck and his friends formed a band, calling themselves the Royal Spades after the highest-ranking hand you can get in a game of poker. They were one of the few white bands in Memphis to play R&B. The Royal Spades performed at high school dances, Catholic Youth Organization dances, and bars for little money and a few beers, just for the fun of it. Their first gig was for a weekly sock hop. Cropper and Freeman pulled together Duck on bass and Terry Johnson on drums. The gig paid $3 and all the fish they could eat.

On an evening in 1958, Duck was at a dance in a community center that hosted events for teens from all the high schools in Memphis. It was here that he met his future wife, June. June told the story of the first time meeting him: "He was very popular and a very good dancer; and it didn't take long to find out his name—'Duck' Dunn." Duck and June continued to date through high school, though it was difficult. The two of them lived across the city from each other and even went to different schools. Between two older brothers still living at home, his parents, and himself, Duck was always the last one able to borrow the family car. Most of the time, a friend of Duck's picked up June and took her home, and sometimes Duck took the bus to visit her for the day.

With no older family members familiar with the music business, Duck's dad, being a candy maker, didn't want Duck to become a professional musician because he was afraid that he might become an addict and die. In an attempt to have a "regular" job, Duck worked as an electrician, repairing air raid sirens installed during World War II. He was regularly late to his job; between the early morning hours and the late night gigs, it was difficult for him to wake up on time.

The Fender came a while after, on one of the boys' outings to downtown Memphis. It was on their way to Lansky Brothers one day that they passed by Amro Music Store on Main Street. In the window on display was a 1958 Fender Precision Bass Guitar with sunburst finish and a tortoise shell pickguard. Charley co-signed for Duck since he didn't have the money to purchase the bass and was too young to finance it himself. According to Charley, it was the third bass guitar sold in Memphis at the time, as the instrument hadn't yet caught on. Although he was ha-

bitually late to work because he went to bed late every night (and Charley would warn him about losing his job), Duck never missed a payment on the bass, much to his brother's relief.

At the age of 18, outside of playing, Duck took to golfing. Charley chuckled as he recalled one of his favorite stories of his younger brother, "I remember there was a VA clinic across the street from the golf course, and some of the paraplegic veterans used to sit on the greens and putt all day long. Duck thought he would place a bet with some of these guys and lost $100 in that afternoon."

A little while after the Spades formed, Cropper was approached by freshman Charles "Packy" Axton in the smoking room, telling him that he wanted to join the band on tenor saxophone. Cropper was about to tell him that they weren't looking for any new musicians until Packy told him that he had access to a recording studio. Eventually, the studio became their regular rehearsal space. The "studio" was home to Satellite Records and was simply a garage owned by Packy's uncle Jim Stewart, with a recording console and a couple of microphones. But as Cropper said, "At least it was a start, a place to be."

While rehearsing at Satellite Records, which was outside of Memphis in Brunswick, Cropper was on the lookout for new musicians to reform the band. Eventually, his line-up, along with Duck, would be keys player "Smoochy" Smith, baritone saxophone player Don Nix, trumpeter (and future co-founder of the Memphis Horns) Wayne Jackson, and tenor saxophone player Charles "Packy" Axton. Because of Duck's other job, he was constantly unavailable, so bassist Lewie Steinberg was regularly at the studio in Duck's absence.

Eventually, the studio moved to its known location, inside an old repurposed theater in Memphis on McLemore Avenue, sharing the space with a record shop. Packy's mother, Estelle, and uncle, Jim Stewart, partnered up and started recording local acts at the studio. Estelle sold records from the renovated concession area, paying attention to musical trends and feeding her discoveries to the studio. It was at this time that Rufus and Carla Thomas recorded "'Cause I Love You," causing the studio to attract attention. Atlantic Records signed a distribution deal with Satellite Records.

In 1961, the Spades were in the studio putting together a new song. Over a period of a few days to a few weeks (there are mixed reports from the various people involved in the sessions), they recorded a number of takes of the song "Last Night." On the particular day of the final cut, Jerry Wexler, Satellite's contact to Atlantic Records, requested a version of the song to include horns. This was when the final recording was probably made. Duck was absent to help his father with a helicopter ride at an amusement park, allowing Steinberg to cut the final version of the song.

Once the record was cut, Stewart took it to local radio stations to see how it would do. There were so many requests to purchase the record that they released it under the Satellite label. Because of the unintentional racist undertones of the band's name, Stewart told the young musicians that they needed to come up with a different name to avoid issues. Eventually, the name would become the Mar-Keys—a play on words with the studio's marquee left over from its days as a theater. After the band members graduated high school in 1959, Satellite Records signed the Mar-Keys.

Charley was driving in the car and heard the song come up on the radio. He joked that he didn't know the Mar-Keys

were that good until he heard the band on the radio and realized they might actually do more than just play the local dive bars for beer and pocket change. The song eventually became a hit, topping out at #2 on the R&B charts and #3 on the pop charts. It would be years before any of them knew it, but this was the beginning of a musical career that would stay with them for the rest of their lives.

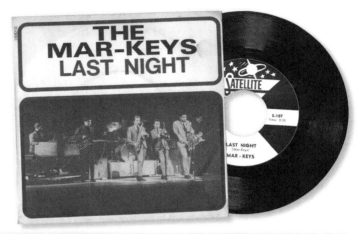

The Mar-Keys – Left to right: Don Nix, Steve Cropper, Charles "Packy" Axton, Donald "Duck" Dunn, Terry Johnson, Jerry Lee "Smoochy" Smith, and Wayne Jackson (Dunn Family Archives)

Chapter 2:
The Mar-Keys and the MGs

"Last Night" was rising in the charts and the timing couldn't have been better. Most of the members had just graduated in June, when the record was released. Duck would say that he just barely graduated high school. Now he was free to spend more time on his career. To get the new single promoted, Satellite Records had the Mar-Keys hit the road. The boys would be driving from city to city, performing in venues across the country.

Although Lewie Steinberg had recorded the bass part, Duck was asked to go on tour instead, probably because Lewie was about ten years older, making the age gap jarring for viewers, plus Duck had fewer responsibilities. "I guess Louie probably felt that he was short cheated a little bit, because he played on 'Last Night' and didn't get to tour with it," Steve said. "We wound up with our high school band going out to Dick Clark and all that stuff."

Estelle Axton, being a maternal influence for all the musicians in the studio, co-signed for a Chevy Greenbrier van for the boys to pile into—eight passengers and all their luggage and gear. For the next two months, they toured the country, performing for their growing fan base. Duck was an easy bandmate to have, constantly telling jokes or showing off his yoyo tricks.

At one point, the tour included Estelle Axton and Carla Thomas, but deciding the road wasn't for them, the two left the tour early, leaving eight young adult teenagers alone with no parents and no chaperones. There were stories of bar brawls, of selling the Greenbrier to fund their dip into Mexico to party, flipping off Dick Clark while a drunken Packy weaved around on stage in a stupor, falling off the roof of a concession stand to chase a rolling bottle of liquor, or Duck pranking Don Nix with a skunk belonging to a stripper. (Note: many of these stories are featured in the book *Memphis Man: Living High, Laying Low* by Don Nix.)

Nevertheless, they continued to knock out fans with their performances, usually surprising the audiences for being a white band, but quickly earning respect with their playing. It became obvious once they started playing "Last Night" that they were the Mar-Keys. Midway through the tour, Steve Cropper left, becoming tired of the shenanigans. Charlie Freeman came in to replace Cropper while they finished out the tour. After a falling out at the label with producer Chips Moman (over a royalty dispute on

the Triumphs' instrumental "Burnt Biscuits"), Steve was in the right place at the right time to become the producer for Satellite Records.

Meanwhile, June waited in Memphis for Duck to come home, working for an attorney to help bring in some money. "They were on the road a lot promoting it, mostly by car. I was out of school by then and missing him a lot, but we stuck it out. After all, they were on a great adventure, and who could complain about that?" June reminisced. The band was in and out of Memphis, often on a short break, and then back out on the road for another stint.

While the Mar-Keys were out on tour, Satellite Records was notified of another record company in California also named Satellite Records. In September of 1961, Stewart and Axton combined their names to come up with the new name, Stax Records.

Stax founders Estelle Axton and Jim Stewart
(Photo by Charlie Gillett Collection/Redferns)

Duck and June got married on January 20, 1962. Touring was less frequent after they married, but they were still out on a semi-regular basis promoting the band. By August of 1962, the Mar-Keys were back in Memphis, swearing off road tours because of low pay, late nights, and poor treatment of the band. There were a few more gigs that paid

Just married: June and Donald Dunn, 1962 (Dunn Family Archives)

well, but by 1963, they were done. Duck was glad to be back around June… and in good time. In September, the Dunns would have a new member of their family—Jeff, born September 17. Now, with a child, Duck was doing his best to stay in Memphis while supporting his family as a musician.

Duck's brother Bobby was a regional sales representative for King Records and hired Duck as a shipping clerk. By day, he was boxing, packing, and shipping records to record shops around the south, and at night, he honed his craft by gigging on the Memphis club scene. Duck would get occasional calls from Steve Cropper to cut demos at the Stax studio when Steinberg couldn't make it. Steve had been working in the Stax Satellite Record Shop by day and recording as a studio musician at night. It was while working at the record shop that Steve met Booker T. Jones and introduced him to the studio where he also would do session work. Steinberg recorded many of the tracks while Duck was working, and Duck squeezed in a session here and there when he wasn't at work or in the clubs. Occasionally, an impromptu session would happen, and if Duck was called, he would put a "back in five minutes" sign on the door at King Records and cut a track.

Every week, Duck and June pooled together what little spending money they had to buy records for Duck to study. "We'd go out, and every week we'd buy Hank Ballard, the Midnighters record, or Bo Diddley, or Little Richard, or just anything that I really liked. And I just played them over and over; I just wore 'em out," Duck said in a podcast.

After gigs, the guys frequented different clubs around Memphis, keeping their fingers on the pulse of the local scene. Some nights, they'd go out to the Plantation Inn, a white club with black acts in West Memphis. Other nights, they'd visit the Manhattan Club, where they would soon meet Al Jackson, Jr., a young club drummer. Eventually, Booker brought Al to the Stax studio and made him one of the core session players. "Al Jackson was the James Jamerson of Stax, and James Jamerson was the secret of Motown, in my opinion," Duck would say on more than one occasion. "I was working at King Records during the day and playing a hillbilly club called Hernando's Hideaway, and I'd stop by and see Al before going home. He was my mentor."

For a bassist, the closest relationship to have in any group is with the drummer. They must understand each other on a musical level that often ends up with the two spending so much time together, they're more like brothers. And this was a relationship Duck and Al would have over the years. They would become very close, and as Stax artist and employee Deanie Parker would say, "I think that the two of them were inseparable. I used to watch them and their affection for each other was genuine." June said, "When he really started his professional career working in the Stax studio in about 1964, he became very close to drummer Al Jackson, who he also credited with teaching him a lot. They were very good friends."

Duck and Al goofing off (Dunn Family Archives)

While recording hit after hit, Duck was spending all day at King Records and all night on the Memphis club scene. He'd swing by Al Jackson's gigs on his way home and then not get to bed until after 4am, despite having to work the next morning at 8. June would wake him up by poking him with a broom. "Al Jackson almost caused a divorce for me. I'd play at this little old, all-white hillbilly club after I'd work at King Records. Al played at the Manhattan Club with Willie [Mitchell], and on the way home I'd stop in there and he'd just mesmerize you. I'd get off at one o'clock, and they got off at four, and I'd come home dragging in at about five in the morning, being accused of being out with other women and this kind of stuff. All I was doing was sitting there watching Al. He was that good!"

Duck eventually replaced his first teacher, Larry Brown, in Ben Branch's band, most likely becoming the first white member of an all-black group in Memphis. He bounced around Memphis, playing in the live scene and working with many of the Stax musicians on the bandstands around Memphis—the Plantation Inn, Hernando's Hideaway, and the Rebel Room, among other clubs.

In the summer of 1962, Booker, Cropper, Jackson, and Steinberg were working a failed session with vocalist Billy Lee (there were mixed stories of whether or not Lee actually showed up, or if he was just too drunk to work), leaving the band sitting around in the studio with no vocalist. They decided to take advantage of the time and lay down some tracks, recording "Behave Yourself" and "Green Onions." Thinking that "Behave Yourself" would be the hit, everyone was surprised when DJs started flipping the record over and playing the B side instead. The band Booker T. & the MGs was formed, with the latter part named after Chips Moman's sports car, a popular vehicle at the time—though Stax would later say that it stood for "Memphis Group" after the British motor company sent a letter stating that they did not want to be affiliated with musicians. Duck would later say in an interview, jokingly, that it stood for "Musical Geniuses."

With Lewie Steinberg on bass, "Green Onions" became a hit and established the band. Lewie would be the main bassist for the next two years, with Duck subbing in from time to time. The catalog for the two could get confusing, making it difficult to know who recorded what. But from 1962 to 1964, Steinberg was the official bassist for the MGs until Duck replaced him. "Lewie was great… he's a great walking bass player. But music kind of changed and went to syncopation. And I was a more syncopated bass player;

it just was a change of the times… it was awkward for me, but over a period of years, we went to a bunch of award shows together because you had to include Lewie, of course! He did 'Green Onions!' But Lewie and I became best friends." It probably helped that Cropper was in a position to influence the studio to instead use his lifelong friend on bass, plus he was playing in a more modern style than Steinberg.

Booker T. & the MGs – Left to right: Duck, Al Jackson, Jr., Booker T. Jones, and Steve Cropper (Photo by CA/Redferns)

This was Duck's first experience touring in an interracial band, with two white players (Cropper and Duck) and two black (Booker and Jackson). It wasn't without its challenges, however. While they were on the road, it was difficult finding restaurants in the south that served both races at the same place, creating uncomfortable moments. Once, the mixed band was asked to order outside, and Duck, being the joker that he was, pretended not to be affiliated with the group and ordered 40 hamburgers. The guys were gone by the time the burgers were finished and had yet to be paid for.

It was right about the time Duck joined the MGs that the Dunns welcomed their newest family member, Michael, who was born March 27, 1964.

As the Stax Records session bassist, Duck recorded with Rufus Thomas and Otis Redding, as well as other artists that came through the doors of the studio. By this time in his life, Duck had been the bassist for "Boom Boom," "Respect," "You Don't Miss Your Water," and countless other hits, but his family was just barely scraping by. "He would work all day, then lock himself in the studio," Don Nix would say. Jeff's first memory of his father was around this time: Duck woke up late morning after a full day of work and a night gig. He sat up, pulled out a cigarette from the nightstand, and had a morning smoke. It was becoming too much. Not only Duck, but most of the musicians at Stax were breaking their backs to pay their own bills while playing sessions. The pay was $15 per session, and if the track was released, an additional $50 was paid to the musicians. This made it necessary for Duck and the other musicians to maintain a steady gigging schedule and a day job just to make ends meet for their families.

Al Bell, director of promotions at Stax Records and Jim Stewart's right-hand man, noticed the yawning and the dragging of feet. He convinced Stewart to place the core members of the studio on salary, freeing them up from other responsibilities and allowing them to pay their bills more easily. This gave them the ability to put more energy into the recording sessions, rather than arrive at the studio fighting off sleep. They were also given a portion of the royalties to be shared with David Porter and Isaac Hayes, creating what would be known as the "Big Six"— Porter, Hayes, Cropper, Jackson, Booker, and Duck. Duck was able to resign from his job at King Records and become a full-time studio bassist at Stax Records. By 1965, Duck, along with the rest of the MGs, were churning out hit records with Otis Redding, Wilson Pickett, Sam & Dave, and so on.

Stax Records artists Sam & Dave record with the Stax studio house band.
Left to right: drummer Al Jackson, Jr., pianist/composer Isaac Hayes, songwriter David Porter, singer Sam Moore, trumpeter Wayne Jackson, bassist Donald "Duck" Dunn, singer Dave Prater, guitarist Steve Cropper, and sousaphone player Booker T. Jones.
(Photo by API/Michael Ochs Archives/Getty Images)

Sam & Dave 1968

Chapter 3:
Triumph and Tragedy

The family moved into a new house in Whitehaven, a new, up-and-coming suburban neighborhood on the south side of Memphis, which was also home to Elvis's Graceland. The move was afforded by the success of the numerous hits that Duck tracked bass on, plus his new salaried position. Home life was good, but Duck was so busy between recording and gigs that his family would only have Sundays to spend time with him. By now, Duck and June had two boys. For the first few years of their lives, the kids didn't see Duck much. June remembers, "The kids were so young when Stax was releasing all those hits, they really didn't get the concept of playing music on a record. So I just told them that daddy was working at his job making money, and of course Jeff just took it literally and thought Duck was at a printing press printing out money. It wasn't 'til they were in their teens, and the Blues Brothers had their hit with 'Soul Man,' that they realized he had played on the original."

Though Duck was extremely busy, he usually made it home for dinner, bringing Don Nix along with him. While the kids called him "Uncle Don" or "Old Weird Don," Duck and June called him their oldest boy. When asked what Duck's definition of happiness was, Don, without hesitation, said, "June. His family. He loved his family first and then he loved his music. He was a good father and a good husband."

Dunn Family Archives

Inside the studio, almost everything seemed to work like a well-oiled machine. Most of the musicians got along with each other, but there was one that didn't get along

with many of them. Wilson Pickett was on loan to Stax Records from Atlantic, and he would cause issues within the studio. Jim Stewart had told Jerry Wexler, producer for Atlantic Records, that Wilson wasn't allowed in the studio anymore. Pickett disrupted the family vibe that Stax had cultivated since the early days of the Royal Spades and wasn't productive to the work they were doing. One day, Don Nix watched Wilson walk straight into the studio while they were tracking. "You know, he's not supposed to be in here. And he had this big red sweater, looked like a neon sign, went down the hall, and he went in the studio and stayed about five minutes and he and Al and Duck comes out, and when Duck gets angry, his face would get red. And Wilson said, 'Hey, if you guys cut with me again, I'm gonna take care of you.' And he tried to give them $100 each. And that pissed them off! He started cutting with Muscle Shoals after that. That's why they called him Wicked Pickett!" After this, Pickett never worked at Stax again.

However, Steve Cropper remembers the story a little differently. He and Pickett used to write together and were good friends. "Almost unanimously, the musicians said he was such an asshole that they couldn't get along with him, and they hated him and were glad that he wouldn't come back to record with them. I told some people like Duck and a few different people, 'Let me tell you this about Wilson Pickett, he's the only guy we ever recorded that gave the band a tip!'" Duck seemed to agree with Steve, having said that, while Pickett could be difficult, he was one of the greatest singers Duck ever worked with and had fun with him. As for the tip, Duck has said that somebody else must have gotten his.

During this time, working at Stax Records was just a place where the guys could record with these great singers and make money. They had no clue how far their influence had reached, but clues were starting to surface. Jack Bruce, bassist with Cream, would later say that he loved hearing the bass line to "I Can't Turn You Loose." The Beatles had already shown influence of the Memphis sound; Paul McCartney's bass line on "Drive My Car" was influenced by Duck's on Otis's "Respect," which Duck used to say was his "one la-di-da."

With the guidance of Jim Stewart, the musicians were worked hard through his critical ear. Duck recalled, "He didn't like too many changes, he liked natural. He sat in the control room, would have his head leaning on his hand and I'd think, what the hell is wrong? We'd be on the floor thinking we were playing our butts off, and he's sitting there acting like he's bored. I thought, are you really getting what we're doing out here? But Jim had a great musical ear."

Stewart's critical ears were paying off. Songs like "Respect," "Mr. Pitiful," and "I Can't Turn You Loose" were topping the charts throughout 1965 while everyone at Stax was working diligently to create the next hit. Besides the hard work in the studio, Duck, along with some of the other Stax musicians, still kept busy in the Memphis music scene. They went to Stax in the morning and left by 8pm to make their other gigs. In the studio, they were working hard creating and cutting hits, while on the bandstand, they could let loose and just play.

In March of 1966, the Beatles were set to record at Stax, and the plan was to land a helicopter on the roof of the building to avoid any trouble with fans... but that fell through pretty quickly (the plan, not the helicopter). Originally, for 50 years the explanation had been that word got out about the Beatles coming to Memphis, and there were ensuing security issues. But a letter eventually surfaced—written by George Harrison in May 1966 to Atlanta DJ Paul Drew—that suggests the reason might have been financially based. Don Nix said, "That broke our hearts. We were all gonna get to see the Beatles record."

Throughout 1966, the "Big Six" continued their joint-producing. Isaac Hayes and David Porter wrote the songs and brought them into the studio where Duck, Steve, and Al collaborated on finding just the right groove to fit the song. Hayes taught the horn players the lines he had created and saved on a tape recorder. Writing and recording songs in the Stax studio was hard work. But working with Otis Redding was different. "When Otis was there, it was just a revitalization of the whole thing. You wanted to play with Otis. He brought out the best in you," said Duck. Otis played the song for the musicians on a guitar so they could hear it. Since Otis wasn't an accomplished guitar player, he played in open tuning, meaning that he could bar one finger across the strings on one single fret and make a chord. Once Cropper was in tune with him, Otis sang the bass part until Duck was with him. After, he walked over to the horn section and sang their parts to each of them individually.

The year 1967 was an historical one for Stax Records and its performers. Things were already going well; this was the year that Duck's bass lines would be heard on

Booker T. & the MGs recording (Pictorial Press Ltd / Alamy Stock Photo)

"Soul Man" (June, upon hearing it, exclaimed, "It's a hit!"), "Knock on Wood," "Hip Hug-Her," "Let Me Be Good to You," "634-5789," among dozens of others. The Stax performers, along with Duck, saw the studio as a place where they could provide for their families by playing music. They had no clue how far their influence reached. But the turning point—the proof that the musicians and singers finally had that showed they were a powerhouse in popular culture—would be their upcoming tour to Europe to play a musical revue of Stax Records…

In the spring of 1967, Stax wanted to debut its lineup of Memphis soul music to the rest of the world, and sent Booker T. & the MGs, along with Otis Redding, Sam & Dave, Eddie Floyd, and Arthur Conley, to Europe on a tour that would change their lives. The performers thought their local brand of Memphis music would be booed off the stage; after all, England was home to some of the biggest names in rock 'n' roll: the Beatles, the Rolling Stones, the Who, and so on.

Duck, along with horn players Wayne Jackson and Joe Arnold, had to quit their regular six-night gig at Hernando's Hideaway. It wasn't a difficult decision for Duck, since he had been on salary at Stax. But Wayne and Joe were not. Having a steady gig made the decision a bit difficult, and the owner of the club wasn't happy about their choice since they had the club packed almost every night.

They started to see their influence the minute they landed in London. Crowds waited impatiently for the stars of Memphis to arrive, cheering and holding signs. They got off the plane only to find a fleet of Bentley limousines, provided by the Beatles, ready to take them to their hotel. Since many of the tunes they were to perform on the tour hadn't been played since they were recorded, they started rehearsing as soon as they arrived at the hotel, tired from travel, jet lag, and hangovers. Most of the songs were forgotten about once the recording session was over. Duck and Steve were asked to do choreography for the show, but they declined.

On the road in Europe for just over three weeks, the Stax acts started at a private party in Astoria and were greeted by Paul McCartney. From there, they played in a number of cities from March to April and were overwhelmed by the excitement and energy that hit them from the European crowds. Doubts abated, the Stax Revue went on to play some of the most memorable live performances many of them would ever have.

It was then that the musicians realized they could make a career out of music, and that the records they already

recorded were well received. For them, it would be a life-changing experience. They were on top of the world. When asked later about how the tour compared to everything he'd done in his life, Duck said, "There's nothing to compare, I think, with the Stax-Volt tour of '67 in Europe. That's probably the highlight of my life." In another interview, he goes into a little more depth: "I had never thought about it before. All I knew was that every day they were saying, 'You got to cut a hit record. You got to cut a hit record.' I never really thought about what we were attempting to do. I never knew how big those records were, 'cause they never let us find out about it. We never got out of the studio! Until we got to Europe. When we got to Europe and found out how big we were, everyone kind of got up in the air about it. That was probably what changed my life more than anything else."

BOOKER T. & THE M.G.'s *Paris, France - March, 1967* STAX RECORD CO.

June: "It showed us how far this music could go, and besides, none of us had ever even known anyone who had been to Europe, and we thought England was Mecca because of all the groups who had come out of there. They were all amazed at how much the Stax music was appreciated over there."

Booker T. & the MGs, along with Wayne Jackson, Joe Arnold, and Andrew Love—billed as the Mar-Keys—backed Arthur Conley, Otis Redding, Carla Thomas, Sam & Dave, and Eddie Floyd. The performers took to sightseeing when they could. Duck brought his wife along, as most of the young, married guys did for this tour. Duck didn't develop much of a taste for the cuisine in Europe and mostly ate boiled eggs and baked potatoes. At one point, he attempted to order fatback cacciatore for dinner.

When they returned to Memphis, the Stax artists had a newfound excitement for recording and worked with even more enthusiasm than before, churning out new records as fast as they could. Coupled with the success of the tour, Stax was experiencing a great period. To keep the momentum going for Otis, Jerry Wexler booked him, along with Booker T. & the MGs and the Mar-Keys horn section, in the Monterey Pop Festival two months later. Being Duck's first time in California, he fell in love with the hippie look and would later grow out his hair and adopt the style. Otis's act looked out of place, having followed Jefferson Airplane and sharing the stage that weekend with the Who, Grateful Dead, and Jimi Hendrix, to name a few. Playing for this hippie/rock crowd were Otis Redding and company… sporting suits. Wayne Jackson would later say that they "must have looked like a lounge act." But Otis seemed to have garnered more audience interaction than any of the other acts that performed that weekend.

Another successful trip down, Otis and the musicians returned to Memphis, where Duck would stay the rest of the year cutting more hits, including "Hold On, I'm Comin'" and "Soul Man." Otis went on tour towards the end of 1967 using the Bar-Kays—a younger band that was nurtured by the Stax musicians—because the MGs were busy making hits.

Otis and the Bar-Kays traveled mostly by his personal Beechcraft plane. Since it only sat eight people, and the group was ten, they would take turns, with two riding in a commercial aircraft. On December 9, 1967, on their way to Madison from Cleveland, bassist James Alexander and roadie Carl Sims were on the rotation to fly commercially while Otis, the Bar-Kays, their valet, and pilot took off in the Beechcraft, ignoring the fact that the battery was low. Due to poor weather, coupled with the battery, the plane crashed into Lake Monona just outside of Madison, Wisconsin—their destination. All passengers, except trumpeter Ben Cauley, were killed.

When Don Nix received word of the crash from a friend who heard the news on the radio, it was reported that Otis, along with Booker T. & the MGs, were killed—not the Bar-Kays. Fearing his best friend was among the passengers in the accident, Don called Duck's phone continuously for about 30 minutes until he picked up, having just come home from a separate tour the MGs were on.

The studio was devastated, and the world watched as the news reported the accident. The Bar-Kays were "the kids" to the Stax Company. Carl Cunningham was taught by Al Jackson, and James Alexander had been taken under Duck's wing. Though Alexander avoided the crash, Duck's 1958 Fender Precision Bass, on which so many hits were recorded, was believed to have been on that plane with the rest of the gear. Otis was like family to Duck and he had even recently attended Duck's birthday party.

According to Deanie Parker, administrative assistant and former Stax-Volt artist, "It went on it seemed for 30 days, because of the time of year and the length of time that it took to recover the bodies, and it seemed as though they were having a funeral almost every day. It was incredibly painful." Shortly after the crash, Don Nix was at the studio with Duck. "UPS pulled up and they brought in all the drums from the Bar-Kays, and they've been in the water for a week, and they were all ruined. They set them in the hallway and that was really a sore." Deanie said this event was like re-opening a wound; the studio was starting to produce again and get back into the groove, but the cases of Carl's drums sitting in the hall brought all those feelings back.

The Bar-Kays (Photo by Gilles Petard/Redferns)

Chapter 4:
Uncertain Times

The somber mood that greeted 1968 continued to worsen for Stax. Otis and the Bar-Kays died only three weeks prior. Otis's funeral, held on December 17, 1967, was overflowing with thousands of fans—some came to pay respect to their favorite singer, while others came to catch sightings of celebrities. Many performers of the time attended the funeral. James Brown's car was weighed down by crazed fans; the tires spun while trying to follow the hearse as police pulled the teens off. Isaac Hayes didn't show for fear of his reaction. The studio and record shop remained closed for about a week to pay respect to the deaths, and to allow everyone to mourn in their own way.

With the death of Otis, the unofficial voice of Stax Records, the company needed to release something as soon as possible. "Dock of the Bay" was what Otis was working on between shows while on tour. According to Duck, Jim Stewart didn't even want to release it, and Duck agreed, citing that the performance style of the song departed too far from R&B. Regardless, it was the most recent track that Otis was working on before the crash and the closest to completion. When asked, Cropper said, "They called me and said 'we gotta get a record out,' and I said we don't have one ready. 'Well, get one ready.' So I went in on a Tuesday morning at seven o'clock and came out on a Wednesday morning at seven o'clock with the record. I stayed up 24 hours and did the whole thing. Otis knew it was a hit. I knew it was a hit. We had been looking for a crossover, so we'd done it on purpose—a ballad thing with that kind of mood to it. And I think, mentally, the thing about this song was more in the groove of the Association, which was kind of a sing-along, poppish thing. And it worked." "(Sittin' On) The Dock of the Bay" was released on January 8th and quickly worked its way up the charts, becoming the first single to hit #1 posthumously.

Just as it was for everyone in the Stax Company, it was hard on Duck, too. "He changed my life!" Duck would later say in an interview. While coping with the loss of his friend and colleague, he regularly had dreams that Otis was still alive. Around this time, new guitarist Bobby Manuel was brought in to help with some of the tracking. He remembers the somber mood in the studio. "I came to Stax in '67, and that was right after what they then called the 'first period.' Otis had just died about the same month after that. That's kinda when I started there. It was a month before I saw anybody there. That was crazy."

Otis Redding, 1967

Steve Cropper – guitarist, producer, and songwriter extraordinaire working his magic at Stax studios
(Photo by Don Paulsen/Michael Ochs Archives/Getty Images)

While things were bad for Stax, they would seemingly get worse. Atlantic Records, with whom Stax had a distributorship deal, had informed Jim Stewart the previous summer that they would be selling to Warner Brothers. After the purchase was made official in January of 1968, Stax had six months to decide whether or not they wanted to be included with Atlantic. After a meeting with Jim Stewart, Estelle Axton, Booker T. & the MGs, David Porter, Isaac Hayes, and Deanie Parker, they came to an agreement that the purchase would not be in the best interest of Stax. Indeed, Jerry Wexler's low offer to join Atlantic in the deal would be called an insult by Stewart. Jim had enacted his key-man clause, allowing Stax to find another company with which to ally. Apparently, both Stewart and Wexler were unaware of what was really behind the low Atlantic offer, until more information would come to light.

In the midst of this, black sanitation workers in Memphis, fed up with job inequality, were in a battle with the city for better wages and treatment. Outside the walls of Stax Records, where the skin color of anyone who entered the front door didn't matter, racism was reaching a critical situation. Inside of Stax Records, however, it was business as usual. Sam & Dave recorded "Soul Man" and "I Thank You." Booker T. & the MGs recorded "Hang 'em High." They had records to cut and didn't desire, nor could they afford, the racial divisions occurring outside the walls of the studio. "As far as I remember," said Steve Cropper, "that there was never, ever, any color that came through those doors."

When things seemed as if they couldn't get any worse, a major event rocked the country and almost directly affected Stax on April 4th, 1968. Don recollected this event: "I remember one time being with Duck; it was about five o'clock and we were at Stax. A singer was there, and it was getting dark. A lot of people had gone from the studio and we were standing outside of Stax. We were looking at the sun going down and talking, and we heard some screaming and carrying on inside, and we went inside."

"Martin Luther King was dead."

Ben Branch, a local bandleader whom Duck looked up to (and would eventually share the bandstand with on a rare occasion of black and white musicians performing together in Memphis), was standing with King when he was shot. King was asking Ben to play "Take My Hand, Precious Lord" for an event later

that night, then stepped out of the room at the Lorraine Hotel. His words to Branch would be his last.

The Lorraine was a sanctuary for the Stax artists, where they went to relax and unwind between sessions, and write many of the hits that would top the pop and R&B charts. The assassination happened in the backyard of Stax Records and in their own oasis. Isaac Hayes walked over to Duck and Don and offered to drive them home; he told them it wasn't safe to be white guys driving home through that neighborhood on that day. Not understanding the severity of the situation, they politely refused his offer and drove home in their own cars. What they noticed on the drive home was alarming: smoke on the horizon from fires around the city.

By May of 1968, Stax informed Atlantic of their decision to part ways. Atlantic dealt more blows to Stewart: Stax Records, where so many hits had been recorded, was not owned by Stax, but Atlantic. Any song that had been released under the contract was included. To add insult to injury, since Sam & Dave were on loan to Stax from Atlantic, they would be bringing the duo back to Atlantic. Without the soul of Stax Records and the MGs accompanying them, the pair would never make another major hit. Stewart would later say that he and Jerry Wexler got into a serious argument, and Wexler claimed that he didn't know that Atlantic had added this portion to the contract.

With no records owned by Stax and two of their major acts gone, Stewart now understood why both Atlantic and Warner Brothers had offered such an insultingly low amount of money for the purchase. Atlantic technically owned every record released by Stax and had the option for the next four years to release anything that had been previously unreleased, which they did… by capitalizing on the death of Otis.

In the last few months, Stax lost Otis Redding. It lost the Bar-Kays. It lost Sam & Dave. It lost all of its master recordings and its distributorship deal with Atlantic Records. But with the assassination of Martin Luther King, Jr., everything at 926 East McLemore Avenue would change forever.

Chapter 5:
Rebirth

The spring of 1968 was both the end of an era and the beginning of a new one for Stax Records. With racial tensions at their height, Duck drove over to Stax the day after Dr. King was shot to pick up his bass with his wife June in the car. There were police patrolling the neighborhood, due to its close proximity to the assassination, and they noticed Isaac Hayes approaching Duck. "All of a sudden these cop cars pull up, cops jump out and pull out their guns. They thought these black guys were doing something to hurt us because we were white." Duck admitted that it was unwise for any of them to have been in the neighborhood during the investigation; after all, the neighborhood was on lockdown. But Duck and Hayes were trying to act as if everything was normal.

The death of Otis and the Bar-Kays left a lot of heartache for everyone in the studio, but they had to keep working. The assassination of Dr. King created a dire situation in Memphis and particularly in the neighborhood around Stax. The racial tensions were starting to creep into the Stax Records family. Al Jackson, with whom Duck had developed one of the best bass/drum pairs in pop music history, suddenly stopped talking to Duck and avoided him. After it got to be too much, Duck asked Al what was going on. Al told him that one of the musicians had said that Duck used the "n-word." Duck said, "Al, if that's the truth, God strike me dead today." Al said, "Dundy Dunn Dunn [Al's name for Duck], what more can I ask?" After that, Al and Duck were once again best friends.

Issues in the neighborhood grew. Many of the musicians used to park across the street at the Big D Supermarket. After King's death, it was more difficult to make it from the door of the car to the front door of the studio without being stopped by someone or threatened in an attempt to extort money. In the beginning they said, "Donate $10 for the cause"; then it was, "Donate $20 for the cause"; then, "Give us money or your life." A couple of men walked into Jim Stewart's office one day, flashed a gun and demanded $50,000. Al Bell once witnessed three men aggressively pestering Duck for $10 after he stepped out of his car at the Big D. Al gave Duck $500 and sent him out to buy five pistols for some of the Stax musicians' self-defense. They were never used.

The decision to leave Atlantic created a surprise that Jim Stewart was unprepared for. Stax, the powerhouse of soul music in the '60s, owned none of the records they created. Even the unreleased records couldn't be sold for four years, after Atlantic/Warner Brothers released the Stax records of their choosing. The break with Atlantic records left Stax without a catalog; Atlantic took the records along with the split, leaving nothing for the company who poured the hard work, heart, and soul into the production of every record. This was a company that had hit rock bottom. Everything changed.

But rather than give up, Jim Stewart, along with Al Bell, created a plan. The first part of the plan involved the safety of Stax employees. Stax built a fence around the building and its own parking lot, set up a security guard post, and hired bodyguards. To be allowed admittance into Stax Records, you either needed an ID or an appointment. Up until now, singers could simply walk in and audition for the shot to be the next sensation. This was now over. Over time, the environment went from being a family to a sterile workplace. "It started out as a family, and ended up as a conglomerate. He just didn't feel like they needed him anymore," June said. "Everything changed at Stax."

Jim Stewart did everything he could to protect everyone in the company. He called the FBI with reports of the robbery attempts, but they didn't help and instead gave him a lecture about the location of his business. In response, Al brought in Johnny Baylor and Dino Woodard as head bodyguards. Without the rapport built up with everyone that had been at Stax, they drew an immediate dislike for Steve, Duck, and Wayne Jackson, simply for being white. Compounded with the fact that the two weren't afraid to threaten any of the Stax employees they were supposed to be protecting, it started to divide the family further.

Stewart and Bell, after the major deception of Atlantic Records, became more business-oriented and organized. As Duck had said, "They wanted to be a major so bad, when all they had to do was just make the music they knew how to make." But, as Duck said in 2009, "We never knew the business end of what Jim was doing. All we did was go in and play. And we didn't know what the deals were with Atlantic; we didn't know there were hard feelings even with Atlantic."

Booker T. & the MGs – late '60s (Dunn Family Archives)

Duck thought that producing full LPs was a mistake. "I think when we started trying to become a major LP in those days, long playing records, and we started producing albums instead of singles; we all made a 45 hit and from the 45 hit, we made an album. We started making albums without making 45 hits. And that's some of my problems with it. It just seemed like a hit album can extend from a hit single."

"Things got so creepy at Stax that he didn't want to go there anymore," Jeff Dunn would say. Duck felt the company had become so impersonal, with so many new faces that simply didn't care to know who he was, that he avoided the studio as often as he could. To make matters worse, Al Bell had recruited Don Davis to help modernize the Stax sound and compete with Motown. It seemed that Davis was allowing the Big Six to do exactly what they'd been doing for years, and he could simply add his name to the royalty pool. This didn't sit well with them, and it drove the original Stax artists further apart.

While there were troubles in the studio, the Dunn family still went on their annual vacations. They regularly went to Miami and sometimes brought Don Nix along. "One of my favorite stories," recalled Don, "is that we'd stay at this really nice hotel, Hummingbird Hotel, down in Miami Beach. We were all out in the pool, and the kids were real little, and they were just kind of wading around. Duck couldn't swim. So June had to go up to the room. And all these people are all out at the pool—it's a pretty high-class deal—and June is walking around the pool, fixin' to go up to the room, and she says, 'Duck, watch the boys.' And Duck's real loud, he says, 'Watch the boys? What do you want me to do if they fall in? Do you want me to go in and drown with them?!'"

And play they did. Booker T. & the MGs had Stax off to a good start with "Soul Limbo." It had a new number designation (0001), and was the first record to include Stax's finger-snapping logo, which would be forever connected with the name of the company. It peaked at #30 on the charts, and "Hang 'em High" would peak on the single charts at #9. It was certainly a positive start. Eddie Floyd and William Bell quickly hit the charts as well, showing an optimistic start for the old/new record company.

With Stax off to a good start but needing to rebuild from the ground up, Al Bell devised a plan to put the record company back into the playing field. Twenty-eight albums were to be recorded in the next year to rebuild the Stax catalog as quickly as possible. The "Big Six," which included Duck, were given production responsibilities, as well as their own offices. Duck, having been influenced by the hippie movement when the MGs were at the Monterey Pop Festival, outfitted his new office with psychedelic colors, posters, and incense. But he would rather be on the golf course. Since he was on salary, Duck went to the golf course instead of the studio. If he was scheduled to track bass, he sometimes sent in Bar-Kays bassist James Alexander to sub for him.

Duck and June sharing a moment (Dunn Family Archives)

As Stax became less and less of a positive working experience, the musicians started accepting more outside work. Duck received calls from studios all over the country, desiring his unique sound. In 1969, Muddy Waters brought Duck to Chicago to record *Fathers and Sons*. "He was really in awe of Muddy and the other musicians who were involved in that project," June said.

With many issues building since the new blood had been brought into the company, Booker had enough and moved to San Francisco, distancing himself from Stax and the south in general. He enticed Steve, Duck, and Al to move to California with him, and they were tempted—especially after Al Bell had halted the idea of them playing with Simon & Garfunkel on "Bridge Over Troubled Water"—but they ultimately felt that they should remain loyal to Stax and declined. Booker continued to record for Stax over the next year, but did so less and less, and by 1970, he was completely separated. He continued to record with the MGs, but the next two albums were his last with Stax. *McLemore Avenue* was a tip to the Beatles' *Abbey Road*. It was the first time that the MGs didn't record an album together. Steve, who was busy producing in New York for Gulf and Western (parent company of Paramount), ended up tracking the guitar parts in Los Angeles after the other three MGs recorded in Memphis.

Stax, having rebuilt itself from the ashes, was again on the forefront of music, and everyone was feeling the financial success. "I'd get on the phone with (loan officer) Joe Harwell. 'Hey, it's Duck. I'd like to buy my wife a car.' Joe Harwell, he was so sweet. 'What kind of car do you want?' 'Cadillac!' 'You work at Stax? OK, it's done.'"

Shortly after Booker's departure, Steve Cropper also left Stax in the fall of 1970. With both Booker and Steve gone, as well as the backbone of Stax Records' rhythm section, they started to farm out production responsibilities to Muscle Shoals (just a few hours away from Memphis) to cover the slack. Duck seemed to be producing more and playing bass less at Stax, but the calls for other studio projects were coming in more often. He found himself less at the studio and more at the golf course. "They wouldn't just play golf," Jeff said, "they'd sit in the clubhouse and have a couple of beers and play dominoes, or whatever. He started occupying his time because things were kinda getting screwy at Stax, and he felt like they were paying him to be there, but when he was there, there was nothing to do." With the better success, Duck moved the family to a larger house in Whitehaven. He also started getting interested in showing horses and stabled their own at a saddle club in the area.

At the end of 1970, the MGs recorded their last album under the Stax label, but not at the Stax studio. The four members headed to New York to record, away from the demands of the company, in an attempt to recapture the Booker T. & the MGs sound. They produced and recorded the album *Melting Pot*, which hit the charts in 1971. Duck and Al later attempted an "MGs" single under the Stax label ("Jamaica, This Morning"), but it didn't include Steve and Booker. The album didn't do so well.

Dunn Family Archives

Thanksgiving at the Dunn home in Sherwood Forest on Echles Drive – circa 1971. Left to right: Tom, James, Jim (father), Charley, Bobby, and Duck. (Dunn Family Archives)

With the growing success of Stax Records, security was amped up even more. Duck was both uncomfortable with the situation and disliked it, even though he understood the need. On one occasion in 1972, as sound engineer Larry Nix (Don's brother) recollected, Duck forgot his company badge a couple of years after the security was in place, and the guard at the gate denied him entrance. Having been the Stax bassist for over a decade held no weight with this uninformed guard, so Duck turned around and went home, saying that the studio could call him when they were ready to record. By the end of 1972, Duck was starting to feel further alienation from Stax. After more than ten years, the company that gave him a career had grown farther and farther from its roots, becoming more corporate-like and political. Duck wasn't even invited to the Wattstax concert in LA. "Wattstax made me feel like I was on my way out, but I didn't particularly give a damn."

During this time, Bill Withers had called Duck, Al, and Booker to record a single. Thinking the song "Harlem" should be on the A-side, Withers put another song, "Ain't No Sunshine," on the B-side. Booker arranged the strings and produced the record, which also included Stephen Stills on guitar. The song would go on to gold.

Later that year, Tony Joe White hired Duck to go on tour with him in Europe. The group opened for Creedence Clearwater Revival, whose backstage pass was a sticker of Gort from *The Day the Earth Stood Still*, with the famous phrase, "klaatu barada nikto" (though it actually reads "klaatu mikto barada"). Duck put the sticker on his '59 Fender, next to his pick guard.

As Duck's interest in showing horses increased, he moved the family to Collierville so they could keep their horses at home, rather than drive out to the saddle club daily. And later, Rolling Stones bassist Bill Wyman met Duck at a Stones concert and stayed the weekend with him in July of 1972, at the home of one of Bill's biggest influences. They continued to be great lifelong friends.

Duck and Bill Wyman – May 2003 (Courtesy of Bill Wyman)

Chapter 6

Elvis Has Left the Building

Elvis Presley

In the summer of 1973, Elvis Presley wanted to bring that Memphis soul to his new album—a sound he had helped influence. The musicians hired for the job included Duck, Al Jackson, guitarist Bobby Manuel, and American Sound studio musicians Tommy Cogbill, Bobby Emmons, Bobby Woods, and Reggie Young. They had all listened to Elvis in their teen years, which was an obvious influence on their playing. Suffice it to say, there was a lot of excitement.

The earlier Stax musicians had spent some time with Elvis in their younger years, attending some of his gatherings when he was more social. But they never had the chance to play with him. "The way we got connected to Elvis," Steve Cropper said, "is that some of Elvis's bodyguards were dating some of our seniors. And the senior girls used to come to these sock hops we used to play and they got to know us through that, and they said, 'Hey you need to come out this Sunday and come out to Graceland.' And when Elvis was in town, we would go to the skating rink or the movie theater…"

But what the session turned out to be was nothing less than a big disappointment. Demos were created with an Elvis impersonator, and while the musicians were trying to figure out how they could put their trademark sounds on the new songs, they were informed that they had to replicate the demos as closely as possible. The musicians started to wonder why they had been called if they weren't able to play the way they did best… and they never got an answer.

What did happen was that Elvis's entourage basically commandeered the studio for a week, and no Stax personnel were allowed in the building, except for the bare essentials. Don Nix was there to convert tape to records because Elvis refused to listen to cuts on tape. No other Stax engineers were allowed in. Elvis's sound engineer was brought in to record, but had no knowledge of the equipment, resulting in an unsatisfying sound.

According to June, Elvis wasn't even recording with the musicians. "[Duck] went into the studio and they recorded some tracks, but Elvis wasn't there—they had another guy who sounded like Elvis to sing with the band. Elvis came in later to hear the tracks, but Duck said he wasn't that friendly with the band—a big disappointment for them."

Duck talked about it in a 2009 interview. "It was [disappointing] for me because 'Don't Be Cruel,' when I was growing up, was one of my favorite songs of all time. And I said, oh, man. Maybe I won't get to play on 'Don't Be Cruel,' but maybe [getting] to play on a hit with him would be incredible; nothing better than hearing yourself on the radio!" After the sessions, there were enough tracks to make a number of albums. None of the tracks the Stax musicians played on managed to chart. All in all, it was, as June had said, a big disappointment for them.

Jerry Lee Lewis recorded an album the same year with a similar idea, though he didn't record at Stax. He invited a number of the Stax musicians, including Duck, Al, and the Memphis Horns, to record at Mercury Records in Nashville. In contrast to Elvis's record, you could hear Duck and Al putting their own playing style on the tracks and a higher quality of sound. The album was a success at #6 on Billboard.

Jeff Dunn recalls: "He had gotten that bass probably about 1970, and it was Bill Black's Fender bass. It's a '57 Precision, and it had a V neck, rather than a C neck. Originally, that bass was black with a white pickguard. And the paint... in hindsight, it should have been left alone. But now, let's say like 1977, and now we live in California. He was on the road; he was gone a lot of times working. It's like ships passing in the night sometimes; I wouldn't see him a lot, but he didn't really know what I was doing. I was taking a wood shop class, and in the class [the teacher] said something like, 'Find something that's old, and made out of wood, that you would like to refinish as a project.' So I'm thinking back then, it wasn't that big of a deal, it was only 20 years old. But I just wasn't thinking straight, and I was like, 'Oh, that horrible black bass, let's do something with that!' So, I took it to school and started doing it, and we stripped it down and put a light finish on it, you know, so it was just wood. And then the pickguard, I think, I don't remember how we found the metal pickguard, or if it was just metal underneath the white, and we just sanded it down. I don't remember if they were made out of metal or plastic back then. That's the one thing I don't remember. But basically, that's what happened. And [Duck] said in an interview—he kept me

Duck Dunn playing the '57 Fender Precision Bass previously owned by Bill Black (early bassist for Elvis Presley) – late '70s (Dunn Family Archives)

out of it—they asked him about that bass... and he said, 'Well, I had Bill Black's, and like an idiot, I decided to refinish it.' And now it's with the Hard Rock Cafe. So what ended up happening after the paint was stripped, like you see it in this picture, we had a friend, guitarist K.K. Martin, and he painted it. He made it into a 'Blues Brothers bass,' so to speak. He painted it a deep, transparent blue so the wood grain shows underneath, and added a chrome pickguard. The last time I saw the bass was at the Hard Rock Cafe in New York City. I've recently found out that it's in the vault at the Hard Rock headquarters awaiting its next destination."

Jerry Lee Lewis

While there were reports of an unpleasant Jerry Lee, many of the people directly or indirectly involved with the project had positive things to say about him. Don Nix said that he "was fun to play with." Cropper said, "He was a great guy. Everybody in Nashville that I talked to said Jerry was one of the greatest guys, but I guess he can probably be pretty hard on people, too." June said, "Duck just loved working with Jerry Lee. He said it was just amazing to see him record."

While Duck and the rest of his friends were working outside the studio, Stax was dying a slow death. Stax security employee Johnny Baylor was stopped at an airport with over $100,000 in cash and a check for $500,000 in 1972. This caught the attention of the IRS, and investigations uncovered many suspicious spending practices by the company.

Further, Stax signed a distribution deal with CBS Records president Clive Davis, who was fired shortly after. Though CBS itself wasn't interested in the distribution of Stax, they wouldn't break the deal. At the same time, Union Planters Bank, where Stax had done their banking for years, decided to foreclose on their loans. By the beginning of 1976, Stax had closed.

Despite the issues at Stax, the musicians didn't seem too surprised or moved. June remembered Duck's reaction, "By the time the end came, he had already distanced himself, so it came as no surprise. It did bring up the question, 'Where do I go now?'" He had been taking outside studio work for some time, though it wasn't enough to pay his bills.

For a short time, Duck kept his family in Memphis, still showing horses, visiting the golf course, and taking gigs when they came. One of Jeff's fondest memories is from around this time, while showing horses: "A mostly happy man who would throw a baseball, football, or shoot baskets with us; he could get cranky, like the time he couldn't get the horse trailer hitch to line up, and it was really hot, and we were running late. He got in the driver's seat of the pickup truck and floored it, doing a complete donut in the front yard, then backed up to the trailer, and 'click,' it worked! We were all pretty quiet as the air conditioning brought us all relief on the way to the horse show."

Shortly before the end of Stax, Booker T. & the MGs were putting plans together for a new album, which was to be recorded in January of 1976. While the album *Universal Language* was recorded and released, one of the members wouldn't be with them at the time of the recording.

On September 30, 1975, Al Jackson was heading home after watching the third boxing match between Muhammad Ali and Joe Frazier. The fight went long, but Ali famously won in the 14th round on a TKO. Because the fight lasted so long, Al arrived at home late—after midnight. Allegedly, Al's wife, Barbara, had walked in on a couple of men ransacking the house and was tied up until Al rang the doorbell. The suspects untied her so that she could answer the door, and when Al came in, he was shot five times in the back—once while standing, and after he fell to the floor, he was shot four more times at point-blank range.

The murder was never solved and remains an open case. Speculation and conspiracy theories surround the tragedy, and since nothing was stolen from the house or Al's person, ulterior motives have been suggested. Rob Bowman, in his book *Soulsville, USA*, wrote that many of the retired police officers involved in the murder investigation seemed to be evading him. One officer told Bowman that things were better left unknown, and later claimed he didn't remember the incident at all. Another officer agreed to an interview, but later canceled on Bowman.

Whatever the true cause of Al's death was, one thing was certain: Al Jackson, Jr., one of the greatest drummers in history—and who, as Duck would say, was the sound of Stax Records—was gone. "It was a real loss that Duck had a hard time adjusting to. Not only was he a great friend, but he was the drummer Duck had the greatest rapport with onstage," June Dunn said. Al was one of Duck's best friends. As Deanie Parker had said, the two were inseparable. "It was like it killed all of us. I mean it was just awful," Don Nix would say.

With the glory of Stax Records over and Al gone, Duck needed a change. He packed up the family and moved out to California, following Booker and Steve.

Al and Duck perform onstage, circa 1968 in New York
(Photo by Michael Ochs Archives/Getty Images)

Chapter 7:
Starting All Over Again

The year 1976 brought forth the biggest changes for the Dunn family. Duck had been through the highs and lows of Stax Records, from its humble beginnings in a garage to its long fall from the top. Stax was no more. But over the years, Duck's playing and personality had built bridges outside of Memphis, and once word got out that one of the most frequently recorded bassists was now available, the calls started to come in.

As Don Nix said, "I didn't care at that time. We didn't care. We all had other things going; he had the Blues Brothers, and he played with all these great people, he was always invited to play on all these great specials. One of them was the *Fathers and Sons* album they cut up in Chicago." The company had alienated those who started with them in exchange for a different direction. They kept them around, but seemingly more out of habit than of preserving the old familial practice.

It was no secret that Duck wasn't too emotional over the demise of Stax. As Rob Bowman wrote in *Soulsville, USA*, "More than one Stax engineer commented that it became obvious that Duck had no longer cared to be there. Although he still showed up for sessions every couple of weeks and still collected his salary, his heart had long ago gone out of a company that he barely recognized."

After Al died, Duck had few close friends left in Tennessee. Booker and Steve moved to California, Al was gone, and Don was often traveling to work with other musicians. Stax, the company who gave him a career and his biggest source of income, had closed, and there wasn't enough work around Memphis left to keep the Dunn family afloat. So they packed up and moved to Thousand Oaks, a suburb of Los Angeles. The family was situated by the summer of 1976, about two weeks before Jeff had started high school. Jeff remembers the initial culture shock, being from Tennessee and moving to California, but he and Michael adapted quickly and ended up loving it.

A few years prior in Memphis, Duck and June had met Levon Helm backstage at a show, and they spent the evening together getting to know each other. Shortly after Duck moved to LA, he and Levon reconnected, and Duck was back to work playing bass in Levon's band along with Steve Cropper on guitar. Soon Duck was on the road with

Levon Helm

the band, essentially starting a major shift in his career—he had previously sworn off touring in 1962 and mostly stayed locked in the studio for the next 15 years. Now, Duck was back on the road, and much of his career would involve the road again, only this time, he was a little older, wiser, and established. This would be more professional and pleasant. "Duck and I had a lot of fun with Levon Helm on the bus and a lot of fun with that band," Steve Cropper said. After a couple of years apart, two of the MGs were now reunited as musical colleagues.

Although he was back to touring, that didn't mean Duck wasn't working in the studio anymore. As Jeff said, "When we got to LA, he was doing tons of studio work." Duck was working a session at least twice a month, and when he wasn't tracking or touring, he spent time with his family.

In 1977, the MGs finally reconnected for a new recording, although they were short one player. With Al Jackson gone, drummer Willie Hall took up his seat. Willie was the drummer who replaced Carl Cunningham in the Bar-Kays when James Alexander and trumpeter Ben Cauley reformed the group. Hall also played drums on a number of Isaac Hayes' albums, including *Hot Buttered Soul* and the *Shaft* soundtrack. He seemed to be the logical choice to take Al's place.

Left to right: Drummer Steve Ferrone, Duck, Tom Petty, and son Jeff – May 2012 (Dunn Family Archives)

While in LA, Duck also did some work as a producer and even produced an album for Wayne Perkins' band, Crimson Tide. During this time, he occasionally played bass for Tom Petty (*Damn the Torpedoes*), the Cate Brothers (*In One Eye and Out the Other* and possibly on their two self-titled albums, which Steve Cropper produced), and Peter Frampton (*Where I Should Be*), as well as other smaller projects. Between his sessions, tours, and royalties, the Dunns weren't in a tough situation, and with the last seven years' transformation of going from the big Stax family to a clumsy corporation (figuring out how to operate as it went and ultimately failing), this was much more welcome.

Levon's band included Duck and Steve along with horn players Lou Marini, Tom Malone, and Alan Rubin. The horn players were also working in the "Saturday Night Live" house band. Levon and the RCO All-Stars (RCO stood for "'R' [Our] Company") played New Years' Eve at the Palladium in 1977, which John Belushi had attended. Just a year prior, Aykroyd and Belushi had thrown together an act called the Blues Brothers and used the "Saturday Night Live" house band for short skits on the show. Eventually, Steve Martin booked a run of shows at the Universal Amphitheater in LA and asked Belushi to open for him. Instead of doing a standup act, Belushi and Aykroyd wanted to perfect the Blues Brothers act.

"Belushi was a big fan of Stax and so Tom Malone, the trombone player at SNL, he said, 'I know Duck Dunn and Steve Cropper.' So I got a call from John Belushi, and I was in California and he was in New York, and it was about three in the morning." Duck thought it was Don Nix playing a prank on him. Don and Duck had a long history of pranking each other and at this point would have been friends for over 20 years. Duck snapped at Belushi, saying, "Don't be calling here now, it's three o'clock in the morning!" and hung up on him. Belushi called him back and stuck with the "story" of being Belushi. "He wanted to know if I'd come to New York."

Duck wasn't the only member of the Blues Brothers who thought it was all a joke. Steve Cropper told a similar story: "I get a call from Belushi, and the first words out of his mouth are, 'I understand you and Duck Dunn don't get along.' And I thought it was a friend of mine calling, and I hung up. He calls again and goes, 'Don't hang up, it's John Belushi.' I said 'bullshit' and hung up again. I was mixing. They knew that if I was mixing, nobody gets through, unless it's the president or my mother or something. And I really and truly thought it was this guy playing pranks on me." This went back and forth in a similar fashion to Duck's experience. Belushi was working on getting the members of the band together in New York for rehearsal at A&R Studios. Cropper was finishing the mixing session in LA, so he arrived two days late to the rehearsals.

Steve retold the story of how he started rehearsals with the Blues Brothers: "The success of that deal, other than the fact that they were so talented, Duck and I only played the same stuff we'd been playing all our lives since high school. Of course, we had the greatest drummer, the greatest keyboard player, Paul Shaffer, and Steve Jordan, and all those guys playing, and Matt 'Guitar' Murphy, and the horns. These were all very talented and sophisticated players. And there's Duck and I playing our same old simple things we always play.

Dunn Family Archives

"I went to New York, and I'll tell you this, we rehearsed at A&R Studios. So they took a car and picked me up at LaGuardia and took me straight to A&R Studios. And they said, 'We'll just wait on you until you get through and keep your luggage in the car.' So I grabbed my guitar and go up to the third floor on the elevator. The elevator opens and Duck is standing right there, saying, 'I gotta talk to you!' He said, 'Man, they're in there doing all this old blues stuff that I know ain't gonna do nothing. You gotta go in there and talk to these guys.' [I said] 'Let me go in there and check it out and see what's going on.'

"And Duck was right. So they'd been up there for two days playing all these obscure blues songs. Nothing wrong with that, but you know, we're on the commercial end. We know what sells and what doesn't sell. So I went in there and we did two hours' worth of rehearsal, and I looked at John and said, 'John, why don't you all do something you can dance to?' And he just turned around and said, 'Like what?' I said, 'Something like Sam & Dave.'

"And I looked at Paul Shaffer and said, 'You remember "Soul Man?"' He said, 'Yeah,' and I just counted it off. I said, 'OK we're doing "Soul Man,"' and they started dancing all crazy, and Aykroyd comes running up on stage doing all his crazy business. He can't dance, but he could play all night, but he can't dance. But that dance became world famous, that crazy shaking his boot.

"Belushi turned around and said, 'Man, that was great and a lot of fun, but I can't sing it that high.' So I said, 'OK,' and dropped it down [from G to E], and it's been there ever since. And that is a true story. I wish Duck was here to back that up, but that's how it happened. The only hit that we had out of that record was 'Soul Man'—that went up the charts. The rest of them were good, 'Rubber Biscuit' and all those things were great, but they didn't sell. 'Soul Man' was the only one that actually sold."

"They did the smartest thing in the world," according to Jeff Dunn, "which was to bring a recording truck when opening a series of shows for Steve Martin at Universal Amphitheater, and that's what became the first album, *Briefcase Full of Blues*."

Duck wasn't exactly enthusiastic about the call. According to June, Jeff, and himself, he was intimidated. "I was scared to death because Shaffer, Steve Jordan… they just intimidated me, and my wife says, 'You gotta do this. You can do this!' So she talked me into doing it, and so I went to New York and it became great. I hadn't had that much fun since the '67 show, and of course, with Eric Clapton!"

Briefcase Full of Blues sold over three million copies and introduced a new generation to the same songs that Duck had been playing for decades. Cropper went on to say, "That spurred them on with Atlantic to put pressure on Universal to get the movie out. And the next stop, it was simple. Hollywood says, 'There are not going to be musicians in this movie. We will use actors and teach them how to play instruments.' And Aykroyd says, 'Not if you want to make a movie with us, you don't. You're going to use our band!' And they said, 'No we're not!' And they butted heads. And Aykroyd won! 'You want a movie with Belushi and me? You're going to use our band members!'"

Over the years, Duck would say many times that the Blues Brothers was one of the most fun bands he'd ever played in—up there with the Stax-Volt tour of 1967 and later with Clapton in 1983.

The Blues Brothers (Dunn Family Archives)

Chapter 8:
The '80s

Anton Fig, a then little-known drummer who had already started making waves by recording with the bands Spider and Kiss, recalls the first time he saw Duck. "The Blues Brothers had played at the Palladium in New York, and we all went over to the hotel. Somehow the word got out that there was a party in Duck's room. Well the room was jam packed with people all going crazy, and at some point the door opened, and Duck looked in and just stood there for a minute taking it all in. Then he closed the door, and I never saw him again that night." Fig didn't meet Duck that day, and it would be over a decade before they officially met.

After the tour, Duck's phone started ringing again. Duck had met Tom Petty a few years prior through Don Nix. Nix had met Petty while working at Shelter Records with Leon Russell and Denny Cordell. Petty wanted to bring Duck back to record a track on his new album. He liked using Duck on one track on his albums, because, as Jeff had heard Duck say in the past, Petty thought, "Duck brought luck."

Duck recorded "Stop Draggin' My Heart Around" at Cherokee Studios in LA for Petty, with Stevie Nicks as a guest, but the song would end up being released on Nicks' debut album instead. Petty still had Duck on one track with "Woman in Love" on his new album, *Hard Promises*. Cropper stressed how much Duck loved Petty and loved working with him.

The Blues Brothers had revitalized interest in blues and R&B with their album *Briefcase Full of Blues* and set out to make their movie. The whole time, Duck was elated that he'd been called to do the gig. "He couldn't believe Belushi and Aykroyd wanted him in the band," June said. "He was a little intimidated at first, but he got over it, and it soon became his most favorite and fun band ever." Duck later said that filming was a lot of fun. It's easy to imagine his good humor and easygoing personality during the long, hard days on the set, with his demeanor keeping everyone in a good mood.

After the filming of the movie, the band went on the road to begin promotions. Like they did with *Briefcase*, the performance at the Universal Amphitheater in Los Angeles was recorded and released as a new live album, *Made in America*.

At the start of 1981, a culmination of successes from the previous year, due to his work in both sound and movie studios, came to fruition. But Duck was overwhelmed with Los Angeles and wanted to move back home to Memphis, which they did. Throughout 1981, Duck worked with a couple of local bands around Memphis. Along with Cropper, he used to visit and sit in with the bands on their gigs, and eventually the bands would end up using him. Duck was enjoying the local gig scene, telling jokes, such as complaining about technical difficulties because the beer was warm. He played with a group called Randy and the Radiants, a garage rock style band run by guitarist and singer Randy Haspel. Word got out that Duck Dunn was playing in a local band in Memphis on weekly hotel gigs, and sometimes celebrity musicians like Jimmy Vaughan and Paul Schaffer would pop in and play with the band.

Drummer Doug Garrison remembers playing with Duck around this time. "He was a blast. Very jovial, fun to work with; he was never negative. To me it was just thrilling. You know how Duck's lines were kinda iconic. They were obvious in a way and super clever in another way. And it was just exciting for me to play those tunes. Just about every tune we did, he played on the record. And it was just exciting to hear how he approached playing those notes. He was very definitive about his lines. It was like the bass line was a tune in itself or something. He'd just play it with a lot of conviction. He didn't mess around; he didn't embellish a lot. He was very authoritative about every single note."

In 1982, Eric Clapton was recording a new album with producer Tom Dowd. While they were recording, Dowd wasn't happy with the musicians (with the exception of guitarist Albert Lee) and urged Clapton to record the songs over again with a new lineup. Clapton agreed and let Dowd choose the musicians. As a recording engineer for Atlantic Records, Dowd met Duck when he was sent to the Stax studio to oversee their recording equipment upgrades. Other than Duck, Dowd called famed session players Ry Cooder on guitar, Roger Hawkins from Muscle Shoals on drums, and studio musician Peter Solley on organ. The band recorded the album *Money and Cigarettes*, which did well on the charts, prompting a worldwide tour in 1983.

In January of 1983, while they were rehearsing in Seattle for their upcoming tour, a tragedy occurred: "The worst day of my life," recalls Don Nix, "it was raining like heck. It was six in the morning, and my mother and my sister came to my house. And I thought, oh hell, what's happened? And they said Michael Dunn has been killed in a car wreck. And I'm gonna tell you, that kid, I helped raise him. He was the sweetest kid I've ever known. And I immediately got in the car, and Duck was fixin' to start a tour with Clapton, and they were in Seattle rehearsing. Clapton

Michael Dunn (Dunn Family Archives)

told him when they told Duck, 'If you can't get a flight, I got a Leer jet sitting waiting on you.' And he was there before I was. When I walked in, we just all grabbed each other and cried. I'm still crying about Mike. After that, Duck changed; it changed Duck. Not a lot, but he toned it way down."

One evening in Memphis, Michael Dunn met with his friends and wanted to head home early. Driving home, he lost control of the car and crashed it in a ditch that was filled with water. An off-duty fireman happened to drive by shortly after, noticed the accident, and tried to rescue him. But by that time, Michael had already drowned, knocked unconscious from the accident and immersed in the water.

Jeff, who was working graveyard shift security at the Carrier air conditioning plant in Collierville, was notified by his friend and co-worker Keith Glover that his brother had been in a bad accident. Keith drove Jeff to his uncle's house, but he remained quiet about his knowledge of Mike, letting Jeff's Uncle Charley break the news. Michael (a talented guitarist) and his brother had played together in a band, trying their own hand at a career in music.

After the funeral, Duck returned to Seattle to begin the tour with Clapton, bringing Jeff and June with him so they could all stay close after the family tragedy. For the first show, Jeff was given an all-access pass. He gravitated to the sound board to watch the show from out front. By the time it was over, Jeff was on the stage, and by instinct, started to pack up Duck's bass and gear. Instantly, the guitar tech, Lee Dickson, who hadn't met Jeff, said, "Hey, you're not supposed to touch that!" assuming that Duck's son was a local stage hand. Overhearing the conversation, the sound engineer, John Godenzi, asked Jeff if he wanted to work with the sound crew. Jeff, pointing up at the lighting rig overhead, said, "I'd rather work with amps and speakers than climbing around on that stuff up there!" And so Jeff, through his dad, got his start as a sound technician and would later move on to become a sound engineer.

Left to right: Duck, Eric Clapton, and John Fogerty (Dunn Family Archives)

Duck on tour with Eric Clapton – Left to right: Albert Lee, Duck, and Eric Clapton (Photo by Rob Verhorst/Redferns)

Duck and Jim Spake with Randy Haspel and the Radiants in Memphis – early '80s (Courtesy of Jim Spake)

Duck toured with Clapton for the next couple of years. Throughout the '80s, he didn't record much in the studio; he was doing more live shows and tours. But the highlight of this period was his work with Clapton, touring from 1983 to 1985 and culminating with the Live Aid benefit concert on July 13, 1985 at the John F. Kennedy Stadium in Philadelphia. They played live for an estimated 90,000 people, and it was broadcast and watched by another estimated 1.5 billion people. One of Jeff's favorite gig stories was witnessing his dad become overwhelmed by the magnitude of the numbers at the show.

Fresh off the tour, Duck returned to Memphis and ran into Jim Spake, who had played saxophone alongside Duck while on tour with Levon Helm and locally with Randy and the Radiants. After some talking, they put together a group including Bobby Manuel, who had played guitar in Steve's stead when he left Stax, and Steve Potts on drums. Called the Coolers, they played a mixture of R&B music, mostly from the Stax and Motown catalogs, while peppering in material from other groups as well. After learning sound engineering on the Clapton tour and other tours with Tasco Sound (the sound company that Clapton employed on that 1983 tour), Jeff was able to further hone his craft by running sound for the Coolers, working around Memphis with Duck.

"That was just a killer band," said Bobby. "It was one great band. So we'd play live two or three nights a week, that kind of thing. It supplemented what we were doing, and we enjoyed getting back out there and playing again. Session work had just dropped off by then. Wasn't enough to live on; those were some tough times." The band performed at the Peabody, which was regularly visited by well-known performers, including Dan Aykroyd, Billy Joel, Ron Wood, George Thorogood, and Joe Walsh.

The year 1988 would feature Duck on a couple more high-profile albums, namely *Crossroads* with Clapton and *Hot Water* with Jimmy Buffett. Jerry Wexler asked Booker T. & the MGs to perform at the Atlantic Records 40th Anniversary Concert on May 14th, 1988. The event brought many of Atlantic's recording veterans under one roof at Madison Square Gardens, and they kept the show going for 13 straight hours. At the show is where the MGs met Bob Dylan, who would eventually use them as the house band for Bob-Fest.

After living in Memphis again for seven years, Duck decided to move to Nashville next, having heard so much about the music scene. It didn't take him long to figure out that Nashville and Duck didn't really mix well. By 1988, Nashville was oversaturated with musicians, and even Duck Dunn couldn't compete. Much like LA, he was overwhelmed with the scene and wanted to leave. His son recalls, "Duck is Duck; at that time, there were other bass players that were younger than him that were playing for a lot less that could probably sound almost just like him and six other famous bass players out there, too." It just didn't mesh well with Duck.

In September of 1990, he took up a friend's offer and moved down to Florida with June. He had met this friend, golfer Mark Lye, when traveling to Florida in the winter to golf. Lye had been living in Florida due to the year-round golfing weather, which appealed to Duck. After vacationing in Florida almost every year for around 20 years, he finally moved there. Duck was going out with the Blues Brothers Band (a group including most of the musicians who performed with the original Blues Brothers, but without Aykroyd) during the summers to tour Europe and would be stuck in Tennessee in the winter anyway, so Florida seemed the logical choice.

Chapter 9:
Semi-Retirement

"My dad was the kind of guy who, every five years, he'd want to move," Jeff said. The family bounced around Memphis through the Stax era, then to Los Angeles, back to Memphis, and then Nashville. This time, they decided to move to their favorite vacation state. Duck, still out on the road with the Blues Brothers, was keeping busy and continued to golf and fish in his spare time.

In 1992, Bob Dylan asked Booker T. & the MGs to be the house band for his 30th Anniversary Concert Celebration in October of that year. Anton Fig, who had met Steve Cropper on "Late Night with David Letterman" when he was a guest on the show, was invited to play in Al Jackson's place. Fig had met Duck the previous year on a Blues Brothers gig that Steve invited him to play on. The concert brought them back to Madison Square Gardens, and the band accompanied a "who's who" list of musicians from the time, including Stevie Wonder, Willie Nelson, Tom Petty, George Harrison, and Neil Young, as well as numerous other high-profile musicians.

Neil Young ended up hiring the MGs to work with him on his tour shortly after and also asked Duck to play with Crosby, Stills, Nash & Young. Duck was usually very reluctant to bring his '59 Fender on the road, especially after losing his '58 in the Otis Redding plane crash of '67, but Neil insisted he bring it and assured him that his guitar techs would take very good care of it. He also asked Duck to bring his Kustom 200 Tuck-and-Roll bass rig, but unfor-

tunately the amp was no longer working. However, Neil asked him to bring it along anyway (as long as the purple pilot light still worked) so they could have it onstage for show, while providing Duck a functional backline.

In 1992, Booker T. & the MGs received major recognition for the influence they had on popular music when they were inducted into the Rock & Roll Hall of Fame.

Several of Duck's awards, including the Rock & Roll Hall of Fame trophy (Dunn Family Archives)

One of Anton Fig's fond memories of Duck came from around this time. "I went to visit Duck one weekend down in Florida, and he said that he and June were going to the store, so I just decided to hang at the house. I saw a golf club lying there and took a practice swing, which unfortunately broke the chandelier to pieces! When they came back 20 minutes later, I had to break the news to them. Both June and Duck seemed nonplussed, and we carried on with the weekend as if nothing had happened."

Duck was keeping busy with Neil throughout the early to mid-'90s, and around the summer of 1993, they went on tour in Europe and ended up playing at a festival with the Black Crowes. Jeff Dunn, after a decade of working as a live sound engineer, was working with the Crowes on that tour. He recalls one of his fondest memories at the festival: witnessing the Black Crowes, Lenny Kravitz (along with his band), and Metallica all hanging in the wings of the stage watching Neil Young perform with his dad on bass, in awe.

Steve Cropper and Duck on tour with Neil Young (Photo by Ebet Roberts/Redferns)

Duck and the Neil Young crew (Courtesy of Steve Potts)

In October of 1993, Booker T. & the MGs played a Memphis music tribute at B.B. King's Blues Club over the weekend. Jeff, who was living in LA at the time, was to start a tour with the Scottish act, Big Country, on the 25th of October in the northeast. Duck asked Jeff if he'd like to leave for the gig early to run sound for the MGs before heading out on the Big Country tour.

After the last show, Duck told Jeff he was feeling weak and asked him to take his bass back to the hotel for him. After returning home to Florida, Duck noticed a lump in his neck, which was a swollen lymph node. He found out that it was cancer, and surgery and radiation followed immediately. This kept Duck from playing until the following January, when he would perform at the grand opening of the House of Blues in New Orleans. Even though he had quit, Duck had spent enough time with cigarettes and a pipe for the damage to have already been done.

After the treatments, the cancer remained dormant for the rest of his life. It did take a toll on his saliva glands, meaning Duck carried water with him at all times. For years, Duck would enjoy an easy semi-retirement, playing mostly with Neil Young and Booker T. When Duck and June moved to their third house in Florida, Duck would call it "the house that Neil built."

In October of 2005, Duck became a grandfather. Jeff named his son Michael, after his brother. And in 2007, the MGs earned a Grammy Lifetime Achievement Award. The award recognized Booker, Steve, Al Jackson (accepted by his wife, Barbara), Duck, and Lewie Steinberg. Duck, who felt awkward when he originally replaced Lewie, sat next to him at the awards ceremony.

Just a few of Duck's accomplishments (Dunn Family Archives)

Duck and his grandson, Michael, on Duck's boat – circa 2010 (Dunn Family Archives)

Chapter 10:
Final Curtain

In May 2012, Duck was in Tokyo doing a series of Stax Revue shows. They were makeup dates, originally scheduled for the previous year, but cancelled due to the massive earthquake and tsunami of 2011. There were two shows a night for five days straight, and the first show started the day after Duck arrived in Japan, giving him very little time to acclimate to the jet lag.

June recalled her last conversation with Duck: "It was very brief and sad, because he was complaining about not feeling well; but he only had one more show to do, then he would be coming home the next day." Duck didn't think it was bad enough to see a doctor in Tokyo and chalked it up to being exhausted from the show run. He figured he would see his own doctor when he returned home to Florida.

The band finished their last show and Duck went to bed shortly after, looking forward to getting back home to Florida and to June. He didn't wake up. On Sunday, May 13th, Duck passed in his sleep due to congestive heart failure. He was 70 years old.

Jeff Dunn has said on more than one occasion, "Sometimes, I think of it as a battle story. He didn't go until his mission was complete." Many of his friends and family easily remembered their last conversation with Duck. June's was just a few hours before he passed. Jeff's last conversation was in late April of 2012. "We went to see Tom Petty about two weeks before he traveled to Japan where he passed. We had a great time and we said hello to Tom and the Heartbreakers. A crew member told me that they never meet folks before a show but they made a wonderful exception for Duck because they loved him so much. The last conversation was we were stuck in traffic leaving the Petty show and dad got a little frustrated. Jokingly, I said, 'Dad, I know you're used to having a police escort or helicopter to speed things up, but we just don't have that now.' He replied, 'Shut the fuck up, Jeff!'"

Don Nix spoke to Duck for the last time about a year before his passing. "I saw him at our 50th high school reunion. He got into town; now, he moved to Florida so I didn't see him much, but I talked to him all the time. We got together there, him and his family and his brothers. All his family ate at this restaurant we used to go to, an Italian restaurant. We all went over there and had a big party. The next night we had the reunion. That's the last time I saw him." About a year after his passing, Nix was passing through Tokyo on his own tour and requested the room that Duck passed in. "Sounds kind of morbid, but it made me feel good."

Since Duck passed away overseas in Japan, the funeral wasn't held until May 23rd, in Memphis. Singer Brian Johnson of AC/DC chartered a private flight for June, Jeff, himself, and his wife, from Sarasota, Florida, to Memphis. Brian, one of Duck's best friends towards the end of his life, was one of the pallbearers, alongside Steve Cropper, Steve Potts, Eddie Floyd, Terry Johnson, and Douglas Massey (a high school friend of Duck's).

Photo by Paul Natkin/Getty Images

Tributes

Steve Cropper

I first met Duck in the sixth grade at Sherwood Junior High. We were fortunate to play behind and with the greatest artists and musicians of our time. Nobody ever kicked me in the butt like Duck. He was raw, simple, and impossible. No one plays like Duck!

Booker T. Jones

"God is calling names in the music world. He gave us these treasures and now he is taking them back. Duck was too close to me for me to, at this point, realize the full implications of his passing." (Written at the time of Duck's passing.)

Michael Lee Dunn

Grandpa was very funny, but I do wish I got to see him longer. I am happy though because I got to meet very famous people with him!!

Steve Potts

Duck was just so special. His heart was just so rich. He was such a great person and his bass playing was just incredible! Incredible. In. Credible.

Courtesy of Steve Potts

Anton Fig

Duck always made me feel good, like he was glad to see me and make music with me.

Bill Wyman

One of my best musician mates. Loved his style of playing which heavily influenced me. I saw a lot of Duck and June over the years, right up to his sad passing. He played at my 70th birthday at Ronnie Scott's Club, London, in October 2006. He was a sweetheart, always full of humor. I miss him still. Fondest memories.

Deanie Parker

I'm genuine to you when I say that I am thrilled you have an interest in Duck and you want to define who he was and what his contributions were. Because I think that he is so deserving and nobody has seen fit to do it.

Don Nix

My sight is slowly going on me. But I'm all right with it; it don't bother me none. I've seen enough. I've seen it all; I traveled the world with Duck Dunn! And it was always a party with Duck! He was a joy to be around, and he was my best friend for all those years.

Larry Nix

Duck was a great guy. The nicest guy!

Dan Lakin

He was one of the nicest men I ever met in my life. He was a true musician: he loved everything about music, he loved musicians, he just said the nicest things about everybody, like John Belushi and the people he worked with. If he had something bad to say, he just didn't say it. He would just completely tell it as it is; there was nothing phony about it.

James Alexander

He was a great person to work under, and we became friends. We stayed in contact with each other, not as much as we probably should have, but all the way up to the end. And he had a great influence on me.

Doug Garrison

He was a blast. Very jovial, fun to work with, and he was never negative.

Bobby Manuel

He was wonderful because of his sense of humor. And if it got tight in there, he knew when to just come through with something and loosen everyone up... there's nothing bad to say about Duck.

Jeff Ament (Pearl Jam)

Duck played deeper and with more economy than most, and profoundly affected how I play with Pearl Jam. Thanks for the education, I'll miss you, DD.

Source: Pearl Jam Bassist Pays Tribute to Duck Dunn
www.ultimateclassicrock.com

Wayne Jackson

Duck Dunn and I were born on the same day at the same hospital. We're both left handed and wound up in the Mar-Keys together at age 17. I always loved Duck and always will. He was a loudmouth and funny and the best bass player I ever heard. In the studio, Duck always had bright comments and funny angles on what we were doing, but he was the backbone of Booker T. & the MGs and Stax Records.

Source: The Bass in the Bass by Andy Tennille
https://linernotejunkie.wordpress.com

Terry Manning

Nothing he did was delicate… every note was powerful, solid, perfectly placed on the mélange of musicality that would place him at the forefront of the pantheon of bass players. There was no indecision, no waffling… Duck knew what the songs needed, and he just got right down to it.

Source: The Bass in the Bass by Andy Tennille
https://linernotejunkie.wordpress.com

David Hood

Duck was a major influence on me… I can't even play with a pick anymore, and it's all because of Duck Dunn.

Source: The Bass in the Bass by Andy Tennille
https://linernotejunkie.wordpress.com

William Bell

He wasn't just a great bass player, he was a great friend.

Source: The Bass in the Bass by Andy Tennille
https://linernotejunkie.wordpress.com

Tom Petty

Duck was just a diamond. He had such a deft touch, and his playing was so full and round. He had that feel that only the best players have. It's very hard to learn instinct like that. He really changed the way the bass was played, and there are only a handful of guys who had that kind of influence: Paul McCartney, James Jamerson, and Duck Dunn. Everyone else kind of jumped off of that.

Source: The Bass in the Bass by Andy Tennille
https://linernotejunkie.wordpress.com

Benmont Tench (Tom Petty & the Heartbreakers)

I didn't play a lot with Duck, but he had an incredible impact on me. There are people in your life that you meet and may only see once in a while, but you have a kinship with them. Doesn't matter that you don't see each other a lot or that you don't stay in better touch, but you'll always be close. Duck had a real kinship with our band, there's no doubt about that. He fit in with our gang. He was somebody we looked up to and admired when we were kids. Hell, we all learned how to play music from those songs he played bass on. He meant so much to me and to all of us. And he was a funny, funny son of a bitch.

Source: The Bass in the Bass by Andy Tennille
https://linernotejunkie.wordpress.com

Peter Frampton

He wrote the book on R&B bass playing.

Source: www.twitter.com

Flea

What a deep pocket that dude had. So glad I got to see him play. Beautiful bass player we'll be listening to forever.

Source: www.ultimateclassicrock.com

Slash

Donald "Duck" Dunn was one of the greatest side and session, blues, R&B, and soul bassists of all time.

Source:
www.twitter.com

Slash with Duck's wife, June – early '90s (Dunn Family Archives)

Will Lee

He was one of the heroes that made up the great rhythm section that was Booker T. & the MGs. Unlike the unsung cats of Motown, this interracial powerhouse made records and went out and performed on their own while they were part of the Memphis soundscape that flooded the radio airwaves, backing up all the Memphis greats. I can't remember a time when I didn't know about Duck. Duck Dunn is a Tennessee treasure, a national treasure, and an international treasure. His music will continue to inspire for generations to come!

SPECIAL TRIBUTE FROM BRIAN JOHNSON OF AC/DC

The first time I met Duck was when I was flying north to do a charity golf game. It turned out I was sitting next to him on first class. He was drinking a bloody Mary and I remember bumping it with my backside and all over his lap—all that ice and tomato all over his jeans! He said to me after I had apologized profusely, "Well that'll wake you up in the morning." It's amazing that he ever spoke to me again, however, we had a great weekend and became firm friends.

Duck and June came to our home for dinners and special occasions for over 25 years; they knew all of our family and friends. I'll never forget one night when Jerry Wexler, another neighbor and friend, was over for dinner. (Jerry produced some of the greatest soul records ever.) Duck and Jerry were talking. Duck: "Jerry, do you remember when we first met?" Jerry: "Yes, you were recording 'Midnight Hour' with Wilson Pickett." Duck: "Yeah, and you told me you'd just come back from New York and there was a new dance called 'The Jerk,' and you said, 'jerk that string once every four bars,' and that changed the song." Then Duck said, "Jerry, did you ever meet Elvis Presley?" Without pausing, Jerry said, "Yup, he was the dumbest fucker I ever met." It was priceless.

One of Duck's favourite musicians, he told me, was Al Jackson, the drummer with the MGs—in Duck's opinion, the best ever. He loved Otis Redding, in fact, he had a broad and expansive view of music and the players involved.

Duck and June had a beautiful old Marantz amp and superb old speakers in his house, and usually at their dinner parties you would always hear the Stax records playing away. He loved rock 'n' roll—Elvis Presley, Little Richard, Chuck Berry. He would sit for a while, then pull out his bass guitar and play along, moving just like he was on stage. Boy, he was fun.

Duck loved to tell jokes. The trouble was he'd start laughing halfway through and could never finish, so

Left to right: Duck Dunn, Jerry Wexler, and Brian Johnson (Dunn Family Archives)

we just used to laugh at Duck telling a joke. The truth is you can't print Duck's jokes in this day and age; he was famous for his cussing, and he was a gentleman of the south.

My last conversation with Duck was the day before he left for Japan. We planned to get together for dinner, on Mother's Day—there would be him and June, me and Brenda, also Jeff, and my mother-in-law. He never made it back. That was a tough week. We just couldn't believe it. Duck was gone, one of the greatest bass players ever, one of the greatest characters ever, and one of my best friends ever, and he was far from home.

Duck Dunn was a friend, but he was also a legend, and every time I met him, I was always aware of that, his stories of the past, of putting his spare bass on Otis Redding's airplane on the night that it crashed—I could always tell that it moved him deeply; they were very tight and had been touring a lot together. But more than anything, I was struck by his humility, the love he had for June and his boys, the laughter and the warmth he brought to every party and every table. I miss him very much.

—**Brian Johnson**

"Turning Goat Piss Into Gasoline"
A Stylistic Analysis of Duck's Bass Lines

Whenever anyone mentions Duck Dunn's bass lines, almost invariably you will get the same answer: Duck played simply. While there's more to it than that, "simple" is a fitting word to describe his playing, if the description is to be only a single word. In the wake of musicians such as Jaco Pastorius or Victor Wooten, many young bassists seem to have forgotten that old adage, "less is more." While James Jamerson was playing his bouncy, playful bass lines in the Snake Pit, Duck Dunn was laying down a solid harmonic and rhythmic foundation upon which the rest of the musicians could build.

Although he was simple, Duck wasn't playing the generic "root-fifth" movement synonymous with the bass playing of that time. His deep pocket further established him as a rhythm section player, rather than solely a bassist. Further, while Duck was accomplished at executing a solid walking bass line, it wasn't Duck's natural playing style.

He didn't read music, but at Stax, it wasn't necessary. The arranger either gave him a chord chart or just told him the chords, and in some instances, told him exactly what to play. Many times, Duck would track the part, listen to it in the control room, and go back for another take, trying to play half as many notes. It's fairly obvious that Duck was heavily influenced by what he did early on with the Mar-Keys, often playing unison lines with Cropper.

Rather than studying formally with teachers, Cropper would say they learned in the real world. "We had a few lessons from time to time, but we were mainly on-the-job-training, self-taught people. Just like a plumber or electrician who never went to electric school or plumbing school to learn how to do that. You learn by watching other people and making things work. You got a drip, you make it stop. You got the power out, you put two and two together, and you make it work 'til you turn the lights on. And you do that enough times through life, you learn how to do that real quick, and real good, but it may not be the way the professor had in mind."

In this section, I will attempt to demonstrate what could be considered a standard Duck Dunn bass line. I will divide it up into three elements that set Duck's playing apart, not only from his predecessors and contemporaries, but also from the bassists that he subsequently influenced in the years following his success. Inside of each element, we will look at a few lines from his earliest days at Stax to his playing in the later years.

It should be noted that, while this analysis isolates Duck's standard style, it doesn't mean that (many) exceptions can't be found. However, if a player looks at what made Duck's playing so unique, this is where to start.

Rhythmic Choices

The most undeniable element of Duck's playing was his deep pocket. His groove centered on the beat (rather than pushing or pulling) and remained rock-solid throughout an entire song.

The bassist/drummer relationship was an important part of music for Duck. When he played with bandleader Ben Branch, the drummer in that group (who was known as "Big Bell") made Duck keep his eyes on the drum kit until Big Bell told him he could face the audience. It was a week before that happened.

As Steve Potts said, "Duck just had a good feel. He wasn't a busy player; his feel was solid… you can't help but to groove with him. You can't help it! I mean it was just so much fun playing with Duck; his groove was just so wide and solid. He was the same from the beginning [of his career] to the end. He never did change his feel."

Many of Duck's lines are syncopated, which helps drive the tune. At the very least, the downbeat of every two measures is reestablished. Duck used to tell the story that Al Jackson (who, Duck would argue, was the "Stax sound," much in the way that Jamerson was the "Motown sound") would tell Duck to wait for Al to play beat two, then he could play after. Often, Duck's first two notes were on the downbeat, then the "and" of two. It wasn't a hard-and-fast rule, but syncopation was very common in Duck's bass lines.

Here are some Duck lines that illustrate this idea…

"Time Is Tight" – Booker T. & the MGs (1969): note emphasis on beat 1, the "and" of 4, and the "and" of 2.

"If" – Herbie Mann (1971): Again, emphasis is on beat 1, but beat 3 is anticipated on the "ah" of 2.

"A Woman in Love (It's Not Me)" – Tom Petty and the Heartbreakers (1980): Duck is favoring the "and" of 4 here.

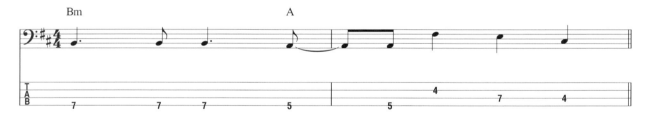

"Stand and Be Counted" – Crosby, Stills, Nash & Young (1999): At the chorus, emphasis is on the "and" of beats 1 and 3:

In each example, the downbeat is reestablished at the beginning of the figure. As a good bassist, it's always the root on the downbeat. His lines are very rhythmically consistent, making it almost a secondary drum pattern for the musicians to depend on.

Note Choices

An often overlooked but equally important element of Duck's style are his note choices. In many of the tunes that Duck played bass on, his first three note choices tended to be root-sixth-fifth. Later in his career, when playing with more rock-oriented bands, Duck sat on the root more often, but still snuck in this signature harmonic movement on a fairly regular basis. Even when walking on "Sweet Home Chicago," his lines would favor this R-6-5 movement. Here are some examples:

"634-5789" – Eddie Floyd (1967)

"Born to Be a Loser" (1974): Duck teeters back and forth between a traditional country root-fifth pattern and his own typical note choices for this one.

"She Caught the Katy" – The Blues Brothers (1980)

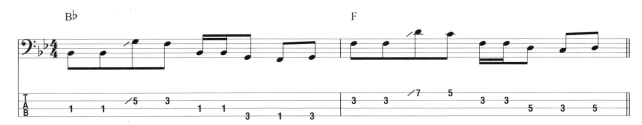

Stylistic Choices

In addition to the rhythm and note choices, Duck's playing still had some extra panache to it. Because some of these idiosyncrasies are difficult to notate in written music, it's best for the reader to listen to each of the previous examples to fully understand. Here is a breakdown of some characteristics…

Articulation:

- Duck's touch was heavy handed, and he really pulled the strings hard.

- Duck would usually slide into the sixth, especially if it was the second note in the line.

- While he generally used his fingers, Duck sometimes used his fingernails for a sharper, more pick-like attack.

- Duck has noted that he sometimes used his fingernails in the studio, but on stage, he'd play too hard and break the nails.

Note lengths:

- Typically, Duck played quarter or eighth notes, giving the bass line a more percussive feel.

- In the early years, Duck's Fender basses included foam mutes inside the bridge cover to help deaden the strings, creating a "thumpy" sound with less sustain.

Fretting choices:

- Duck was not afraid to use open strings in his bass lines; if it was much easier using open strings, he would do so.

- That being said, Duck would also say that notes sounded "better" when played on a lower string because of the deeper timbre of the thicker string.

- As noted above, when going for the sixth, Duck would generally slide into it.

In addition to the above, one cannot forget about the equipment that Duck used to achieve his famous sound…

Equipment

In a time when many freelance/session bassists collected a multitude of basses to chase after the sounds required by the bandleader, Duck was simple. While he did experiment with different basses over the years, he still went for that same signature tone.

Despite everything mentioned in this section, Duck felt that it wasn't the gear that made the musician. Jeff said, "He didn't care what it was, as long as the gear is in working order. The sound is in the fingers." So, while this is a look at the instruments Duck Dunn used, it doesn't mean he believed the instrument makes the player, in fact, he believed quite the opposite.

"The first [bass] I had was a Kay, I believe," Duck told Willie Moseley in a 2006 interview. That bass was most likely the K-162 Electronic Bass, which was the second most mass-produced bass guitar, after the Fender Precision.

Duck's brother co-signed to help purchase his first Fender bass (which replaced his Kay), since he was too young to buy his own. From then on, Duck was hooked on Fender basses. That first Fender Precision was a 1958 Fender P-Bass with a sunburst finish, rosewood fretboard, and tortoise shell pickguard. This was the instrument he ended up playing with the Mar-Keys. The bass may have gone down in December of 1967 in Otis Redding's plane crash, but since it was James Alexander's turn to fly in a different plane that day, the bass may have survived with him.

Duck's second bass was a Fender 1959 Fender Precision with a sunburst finish, maple fretboard, and gold anodized pickguard. This is the bass he is most well-known for. It was thought to be a 1958 Precision, but when it was having some work done in 2015, the date "4–59" was found handwritten on the heel. It has a little extender at the end of the E string on the bridge, so the jagged winding on the end of the string isn't a part of the overall string length, which is thought to improve sound and intonation.

Duck also owned a 1966 Fender P-Bass with a red body, rosewood fretboard, and white pickguard. This bass can be seen in the Holiday Inn/Murph and the Magic Tones scene in *The Blues Brothers* movie. When he later took this bass in for repairs, he was told the neck was bowed, so he bought a Jazz Bass neck that was sitting in the corner of the shop and had the tech swap the necks out. The neck was from a 1970s Fender Jazz Bass with a rosewood fingerboard and block inlays.

Early Fender basses came stocked with a bridge cover that included a foam mute to help dampen the strings. Duck utilized these mutes on his early recordings, but eventually removed them around 1968–1970, as music styles and requirements changed.

In 1998, Fender made a limited edition Duck Dunn Signature Bass. The instrument was based on the design of the 1959 Precision, with a red body, gold anodized pickguard, and maple neck. The nut width is 1⅝" rather than the 1¾" nut width of the '59, because Duck was getting into skinnier necks at the time; he felt that they were easier to play as he was getting older. Fender made just under 300 units, and the bass was crafted in Japan.

In 2005–2006, Dan Lakin of Lakland Basses made Duck a bass. It was based on Duck's 1966 Precision. Dubbed the "Duck Dunn Model," it gave consumers a larger variety of color options. The instrument looked much like his '66, with a red body, rosewood fretboard, and block inlays. After Dan Lakin left the company, Lakland kept the model, but changed the designation, distancing it from Duck's affiliation.

"He dabbled with some other brands like Yamaha and Peavey and had some unique basses. But for getting business done, he always went back to Fender or Lakland," Jeff said. Indeed, while the odd picture can be seen where he's holding something different, the majority of the time, he played only Fender Precision basses until Dan Lakin made him his Lakland Duck Dunn Signature Bass.

Courtesy of Fender

Kay K-162 Electronic Bass, the model Duck probably played before he bought his first Fender bass (Photo courtesy of Cream City Music)

1958 Fender Precision Bass on display at the Stax Museum. It's possible that this was Duck's first Fender. (Courtesy of Stax Museum, Memphis, TN)

The 1959 Fender Precision Bass that became synonymous with Duck Dunn (Dunn Family Archives/ Manny Cruz)

Duck's 1966 Fender Precision Bass with a Jazz neck that he had installed later. Both the body and original neck have "demo" stamped on the back. (Dunn Family Archives/ Manny Cruz)

Fender Duck Dunn Signature Bass. This is the one Duck used in the Blues Brothers 2000 movie, and is serial number 0001. (Dunn Family Archives/ Manny Cruz)

Duck's Lakland Signature bass, strongly resembling his red Fender '66 (Dunn Family Archives/ Manny Cruz)

43

Like most of his contemporaries, Duck always used La-Bella 760 flatwound strings on all of his basses. He never changed his strings until one broke, then he would replace the entire set. His belief was that flatwounds improved over time.

While his choice in instruments seemed to come from deep personal ideals of what a bass should be, his choice in amplification was less involved. In the studio, Duck used an Ampeg B-15 Flip Top, but he actually wasn't a fan of its live sound. He felt that it sounded "thin" while playing, but after hearing the resulting recordings, felt it sounded "right." Inside the Stax studio, the Altec speakers that came with the purchased theater were repurposed as studio monitors for the recording sessions. Since the bass is usually connected directly to the console along with the amp, the studio amplifier wasn't such an important detail to Duck.

On the '67 Europe tour, Marshall equipment was utilized. Again, since Duck wasn't picky on amplification, he took whatever backline was provided for him. On live shows, Duck preferred a Kustom 200 Black Tuck-and-Roll, along with two 2x15 matching Kustom cabinets loaded with JBL speakers. Neil Young loved the amp so much that, even when it wasn't working, he still asked Duck to use it onstage as long as the power light would illuminate. They had another amp on stage for monitoring.

Later in Duck's life, he was endorsed by Ampeg and used various Ampeg SVT amplifiers, depending on what backline companies had to offer. He was a fan of Ampeg's 8x10 speaker cabinets.

Duck was very tone conscious and didn't like it if the bass was "too bassy." He felt that if the bass tone was too dark, it would sound undefined and lose the punch.

Duck had other basses besides Fender, but they were largely collectibles or gifts given to him by friends. He preferred his Fender basses, until Dan Lakin made him a bass with a thinner neck, which was easier on his hands. The white binding on the side of the neck made it easier to see the fret marks in low-light situations.

If you asked Duck about effects, he would have said his favorite two are the pipe he occasionally smoked while playing, and the 1/4" instrument cable that connected his bass to the amp or recording console. If there was one thing that Duck used to tailor his sound, it would have been where he positioned the tone knob, depending on the bass, to find the sweet spot in the sound, rather than turning it all the way up. As far as the volume knob goes, it would almost always be full up on the bass.

Ampeg B-15 Bass Amplifier
(Courtesy of Ampeg)

Ampeg SVT Bass Amplifier
(Courtesy of Ampeg)

Courtesy of Ampeg

Museum Tour

Here are some of Duck's basses, on display at
various museums and exhibits around the U.S.

*1951 Fender Precision (debut year of the
Precision—only about 83 were made)
from Duck's personal collection, located
at the Rock & Roll Hall of Fame in the
"Respect the Sound of Soul" exhibit
(Photo by dpi digital content, courtesy
of the Rock & Roll Hall of Fame)*

Duck Dunn exhibit at the Hard Rock Café in Orlando, Florida

DONALD "DUCK" DUNN
BOOKER T. & THE MG'S

AS THE BASSIST FOR BOOKER T. & THE MG'S, AND FOR OTHER
LEGENDARY STAX ARTISTS, DONALD "DUCK" DUNN BECAME
THE MAN WHO PROVIDED A GROOVE FOR AN ENTIRE GENERATION
TO DANCE TO. THIS BASS, DESIGNED BY DUNN WAS USED IN THE
"BLUES BROTHERS 2000" MOVIE.

In the summer of 1998, during the filming of *Blues Brothers 2000*, the red Fender Duck Dunn Precision basses
were about to be introduced. Duck wished to use the model in the movie, so Fender gave him #0001 and
#0002. Duck kept #0001 for himself, and he used #0002 for the movie during the "Ghost Riders in the Sky"
rainstorm scene. So after it had a shower, it became a part of the Hard Rock Café's collection. The third bass
(#0003) came later and was a 36th birthday present to Duck's son Jeff. Jeff removed the lacquer from the back
of the neck and installed a Hipshot "D" tuner.

The Bass Lines of Duck Dunn

I have to admit, I'm not much of an author. I was the student who barely passed my English composition classes so I could spend more time in the practice room. Like many musicians, I would rather let the music do the talking, than talk about the music. When I discovered that there was very little information published about Duck, I set out to do my own personal study, but decided that this was something that should be shared. Furthermore, I would never have had the opportunity to go so deep into my research without an official reason to call Duck's old "war buddies." Everyone I've talked to about Duck had so much to say, and while it made the biography portion easier, the transcriptions are where I'm more comfortable.

While talking to the many musicians about Duck, Will Lee flat-out asked if he could be a part of the recording, and I immediately sent him the list of tracks and told him to take his pick. Of course, Will sounds great on his two tracks, and I am forever grateful to him for participating.

Will Lee, recording "Hip Hug-Her" for this book in Erik Eldenius' studio – March 2017

Here and there, some of the following bass lines have been transcribed in other publications with varying accuracy. I've spent an inordinate amount of time on them, trying to catch every inflection that might have been recorded. What follows are the result of hours of painstaking study, and hopefully, the most accurate transcriptions to date. Of course, the best teacher is Duck himself, so be sure to listen to his original recordings for the real deal!

While some bass lines are flashier and some are simpler, it was the feel that governed what to play. Sometimes, Duck did make mistakes, but it was how he got back on the figurative "horse" that further proves his competence as a session bassist. He never lost the feel, and unless you're studying the bass part intently (such as when studying these transcriptions), you'd never have noticed.

About the Audio

The 28 audio tracks that accompany this book can be accessed by visiting **www.halleonard.com/mylibrary** and entering the code found on page 1.

All tracks are mixed with the bass alone on the left channel and everything else on the right channel. You can opt to listen to the isolated bass, to hear exactly what Duck played on those tracks, or you can listen to the band without the bass, allowing you to play along with the other musicians on the track. Of course, you can also listen to the mix as a whole. When accessing the tracks online, you can adjust the balance control using the **PLAYBACK+** audio player, allowing you to pan the channels left or right for the mix you desire.

 This icon indicates that a song has an audio track.

Will playing Duck's '59 at the Capitol Theatre, Clearwater, FL – March 4th, 2017 (Dunn Family Archives)

Recording Credits:

Nick

Chris

Steve

Jeff

Bob

Magic Alex

The basses that were used in the recordings for the book – Duck's bass (rear left), and Nick's main Precision (front center), are featured on the majority of the recordings

Will Lee – Bass on "634-5789" (Wilson Pickett) and "Hip Hug-Her"
Jeff Dunn – Bass on "Soul Man"
Nick Rosaci – Bass on all remaining tracks
Chris Peet – Drums
Steve Laudicina – Guitar
Bob Taylor – Keys
Alex Saenz – Engineer

Recorded Monday, January 30 through Wednesday, February 1
at Legacy Sound Studio in Wellington, Florida (www.legacysoundstudio.com).

All tracks performed, recorded, and mixed by the above list of players, except backing tracks for "Last Night,"
"In the Midnight Hour," "I Thank You," "Soul Man," and "Crosscut Saw" provided by Hal Leonard.

Many of the tracks were performed on Duck's original '59 Fender Precision Bass.

Last Night

It should be noted that it was most definitely Lewie Steinberg who played on this record. The song took anywhere from two weeks to a month to record, depending on who was asked. On the day that this fateful recording was most likely made, Duck had to go out and help his dad with a helicopter ride for kids—the kind of stuff you'd see at a carnival. Duck probably missed the take that would end up getting pressed. That being said, Duck had played this tune more times than Lewie ever did, and since it was the tune that started Duck's career, it seems fitting to include it.

The Mar-Keys
Single, 1961

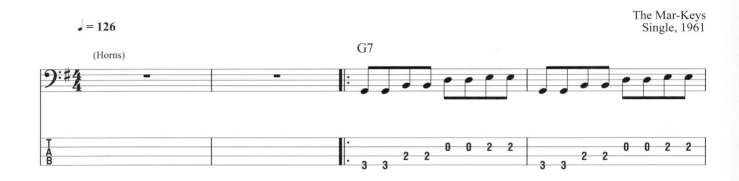

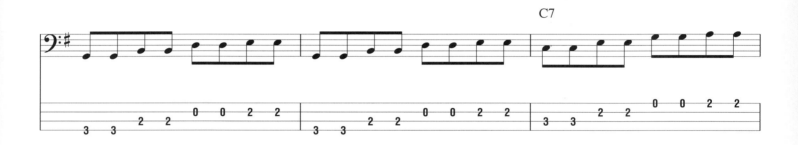

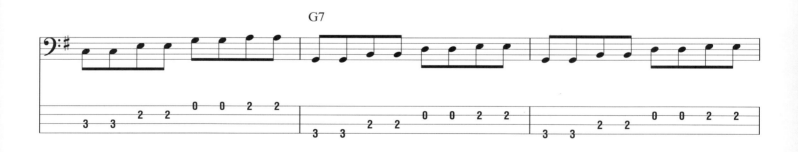

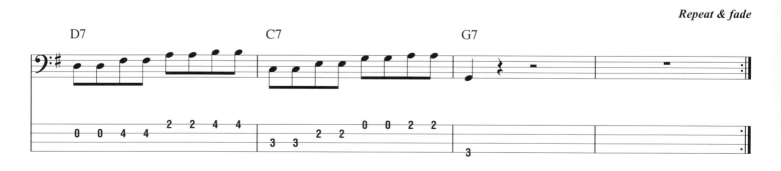

You Don't Miss Your Water

Duck really kept this bass line simple. He tended to play roots and walked from one note to the next. Be careful with the ends of the notes, as well as the beginnings—keep in mind where Duck is cutting off each note.

William Bell
Single, 1961

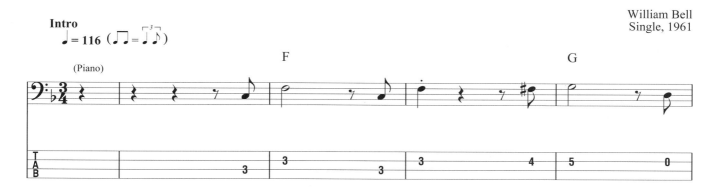

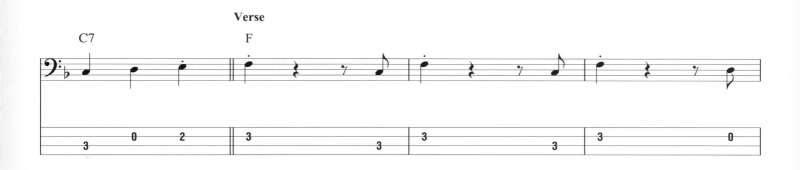

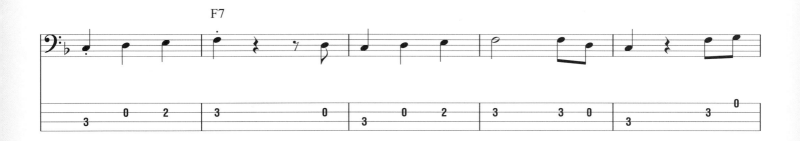

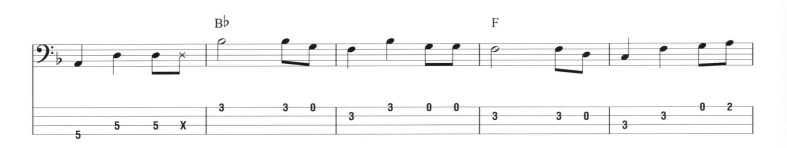

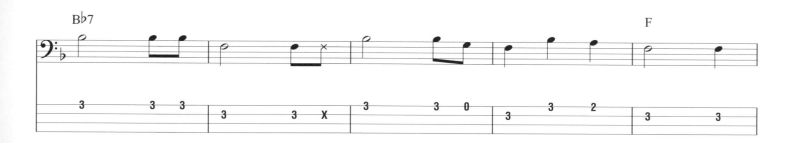

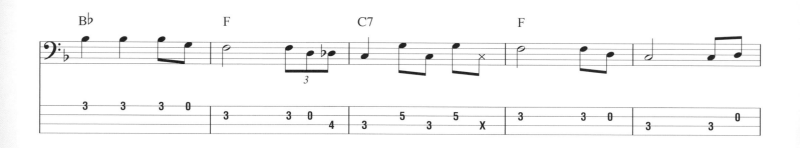

To Next Verse

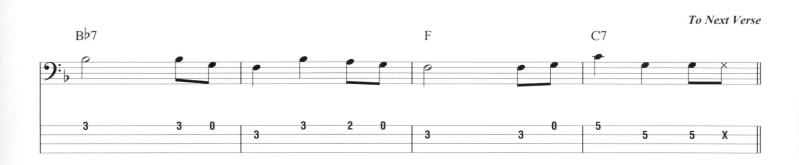

Boom Boom

Duck used to say that Lewie was the better walker, and that he was the better syncopated bassist. But make no mistake, his walking bass lines were solid and in the pocket. He was more repetitive on this particular song, but the line serves the song, rather than the bass.

Rufus Thomas
Walking the Dog, 1964

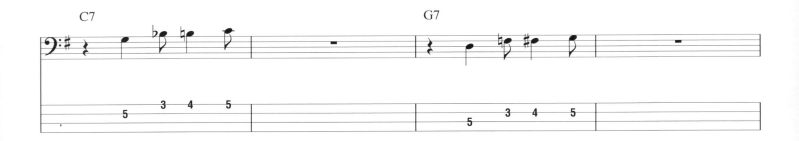

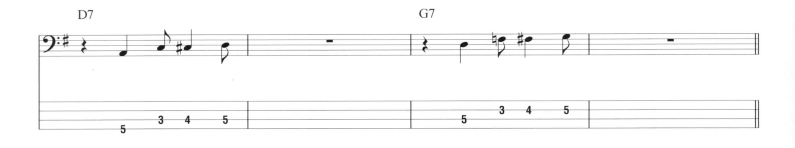

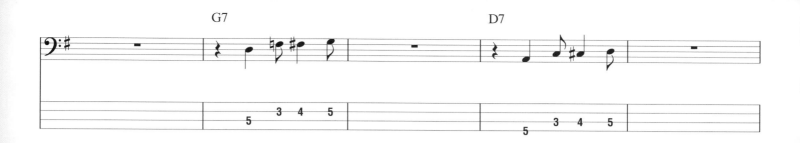

Chorus

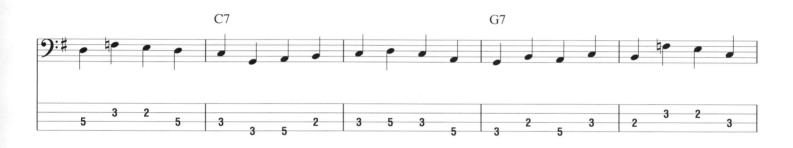

Verse

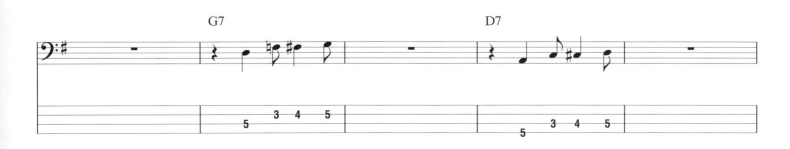

Sax Solo

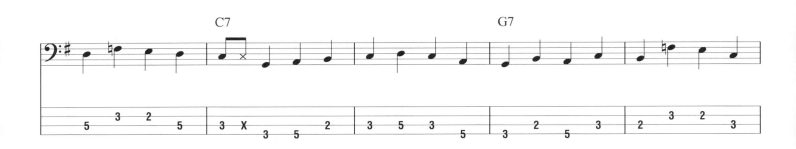

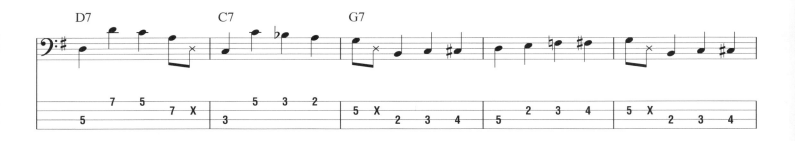

Outro-Chorus

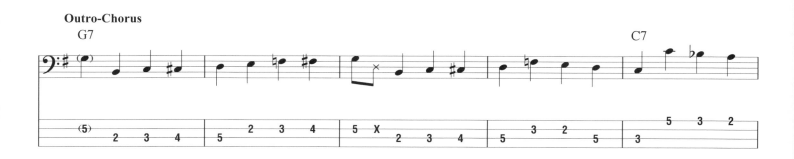

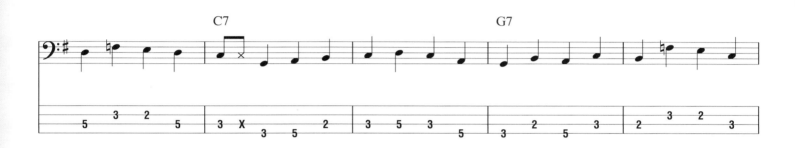

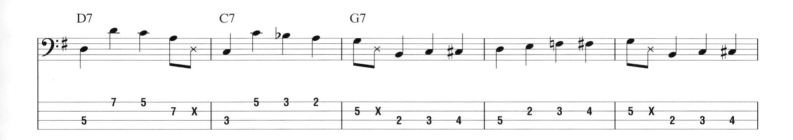

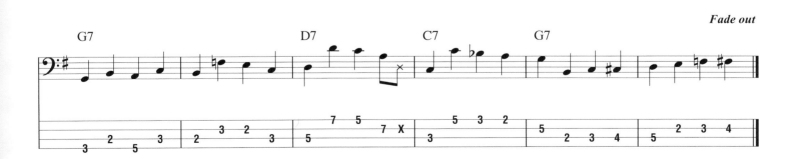

These Arms of Mine

This was the song that Otis Redding sang for his Stax audition. In Robert Gordon's book, *Respect Yourself*, Steve Cropper said that he called Lewie Steinberg to track the bass part. When I asked Steve, he said, "Well, Duck told me—I always thought it was Lewie. And I think Duck heard me say that one time in an interview or something. And he said, 'Crop, that was me playing!' And I said, 'It was?' And he said, 'Yeah, don't you remember come running out on the sidewalk and I was putting my bass in the trunk, and you said, "Get your bass out, we got another track to cut"?' And I said, 'Well, golly, I guess so!'"

In this song, Duck tends to outline the triads in a repetitive rhythm. Again, little attention is brought to the bass.

Grab This Thing

This is around the time that Duck's syncopation seems to start. The tune was actually pressed on both sides of the record due to length, and Duck gets a rare opportunity to play a solo, weaving in and out of Al Jackson's drumming.

The Mar-Keys
Single, 1965

Words and Music by Steve Cropper and Al Bell
Copyright © 1965 IRVING MUSIC, INC.
Copyright Renewed
All Rights Reserved   Used by Permission

Respect

Duck's line in this tune is bouncy and mostly arpeggiated. The bass line was used in the Beatles song "Drive My Car," to which Duck said, "That's my one la-di-da."

There are many transcriptions of this bass line floating around, but none of them seem to accurately capture the bridge. Duck doesn't just play quarter notes on the root. As he would often do, Duck avoids beat 2, letting Al hit it before continuing the rest of the bass line. What Duck actually played was funkier than he was given credit for.

Otis Redding
Single, 1965

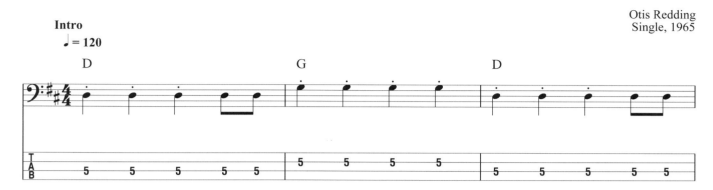

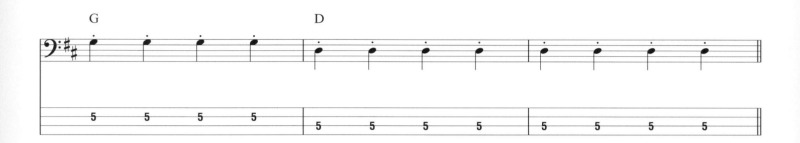

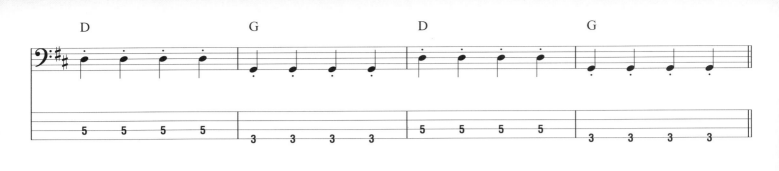

Verse

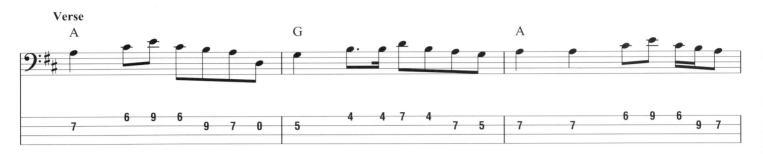

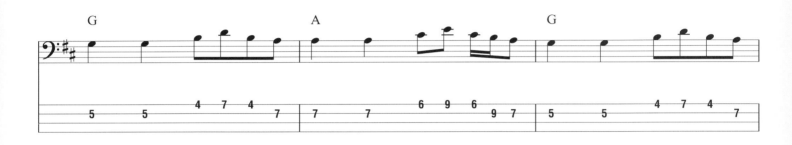

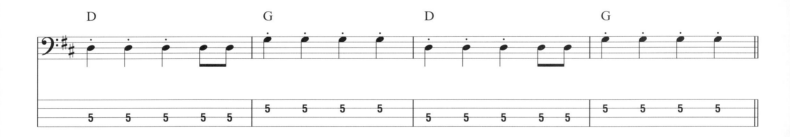

Bridge

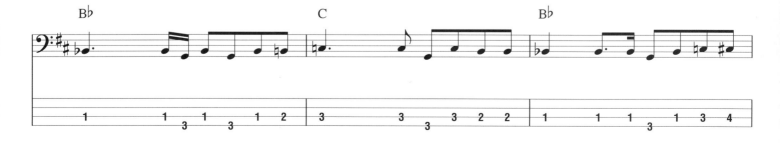

I Can't Turn You Loose

Duck and Steve, for the most part, played the same line in octaves for this tune, as they did for many. The root-sixth-fifth movement is prevalent in this line and would later start to develop into Duck's signature note choices.

Otis Redding
Single, 1965

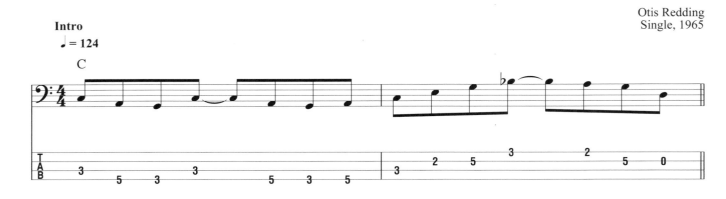

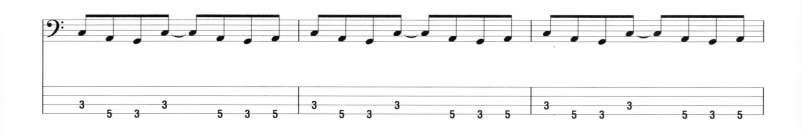

In the Midnight Hour

Jerry Wexler visited the studio at the time this tune was to be recorded. He said that there was a new dance in New York called "The Jerk" and showed them the dance. It accented the backbeat—beats 2 and 4—which Al and Duck emphasized. So, Jerry Wexler essentially wrote the groove for this tune. The song made it to #1 on the charts in 1965.

Wilson Pickett
Single, 1965

Mr. Pitiful

Duck avoids beat 2 throughout the song, and instead of playing the "and" of 2, he plays the "ah," giving the groove a snappier feel.

Otis Redding
The Great Otis Redding Sings Soul Ballads, 1965

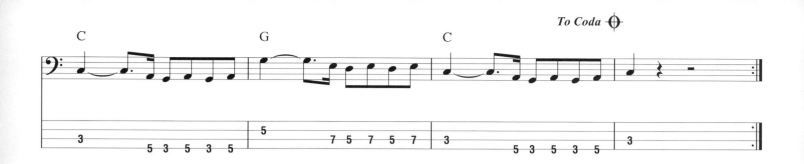

Interlude

Bridge

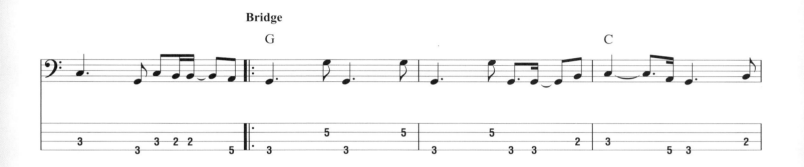

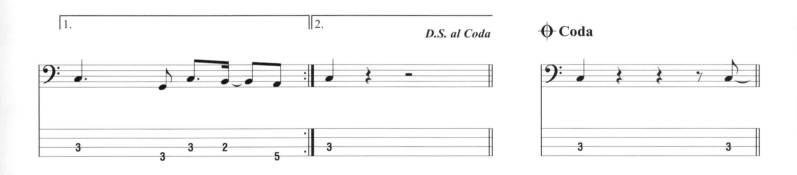

Outro

*Not tied on repeats

You Don't Know Like I Know

This hit put Sam & Dave on the charts for the first time, even though Sam Moore wasn't a fan of the song. He didn't like the aggressive feel that Hayes and Porter were having him do, but it seemed to work.

While Duck does avoid beat 2 in the chorus, he plays on that beat during the verse and bridge, essentially reinforcing what Al Jackson is doing on the drums. The driving eighth-note run at the outro is particularly fun—changing only one note between each chord.

Sam & Dave
Single, 1965

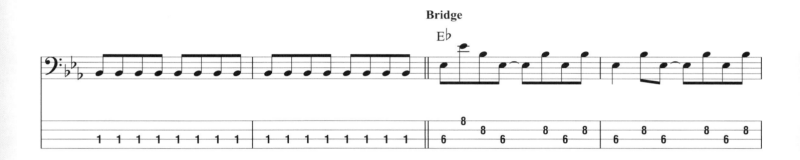

Bridge

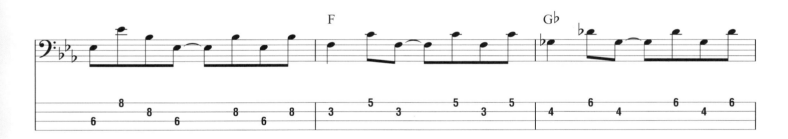

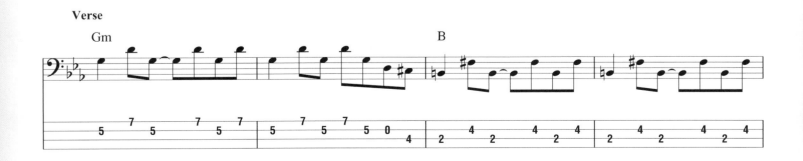

Let Me Be Good to You

Carla Thomas
Single, 1966

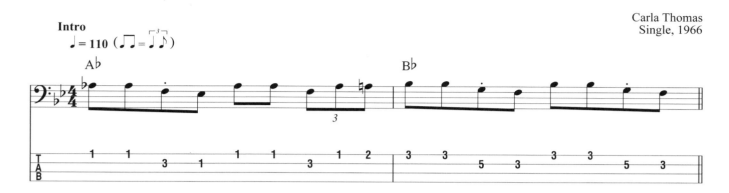

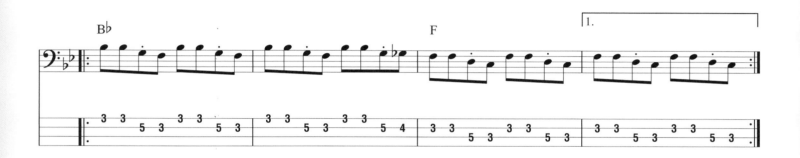

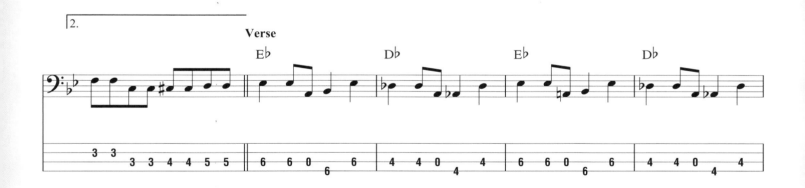

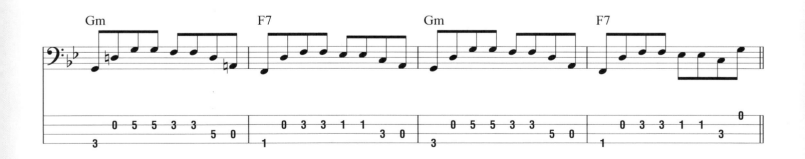

Chorus

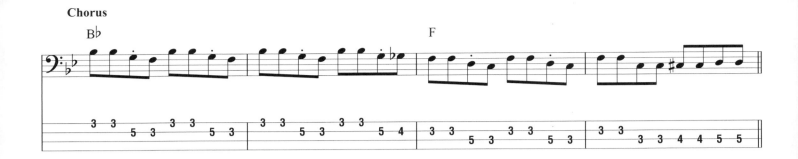

Verse

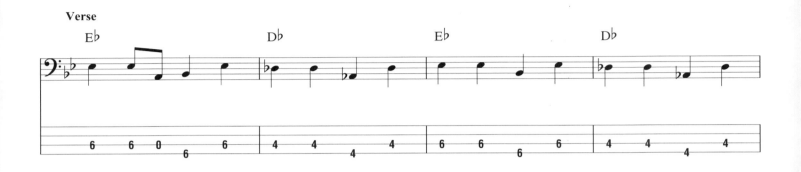

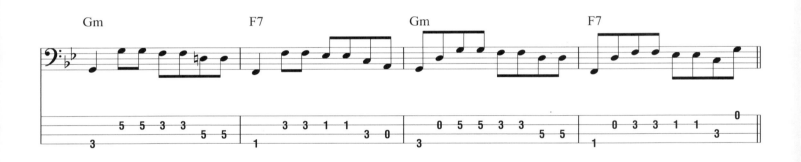

Chorus

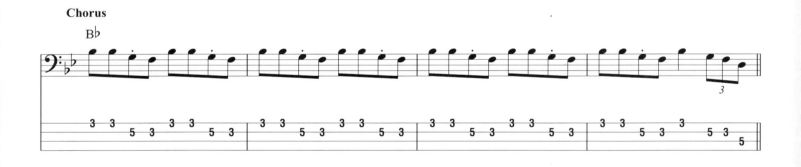

Bridge

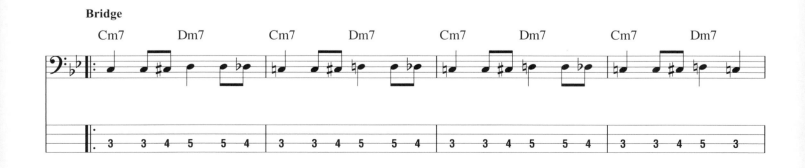

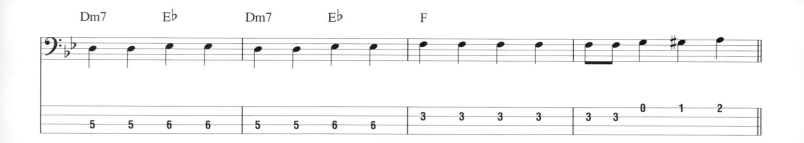

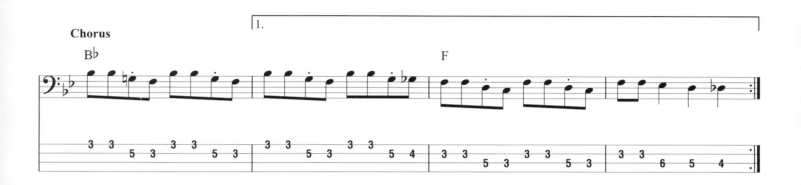

Chorus

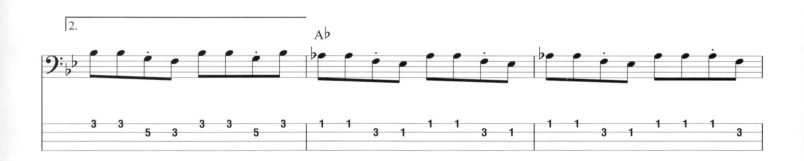

Outro

Repeat & fade

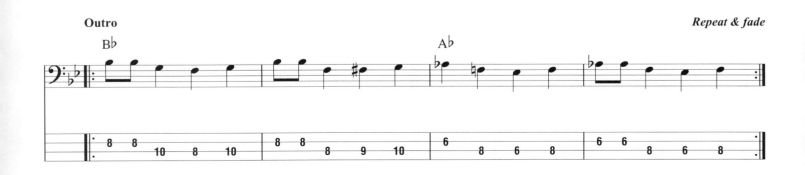

B-A-B-Y

Duck keeps the rhythmic pattern consistent from measure to measure during the verses while using the typical root-sixth-fifth movement.

Carla Thomas
Carla, 1966

But It's Alright

Eddie Floyd
Knock on Wood, 1967

Pre-Chorus

Outro-Chorus

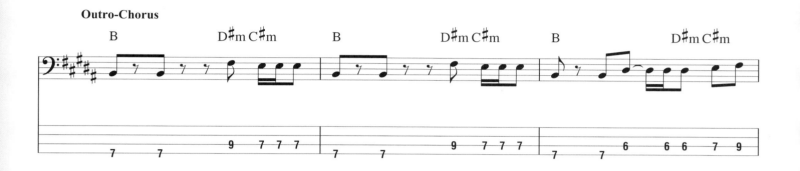

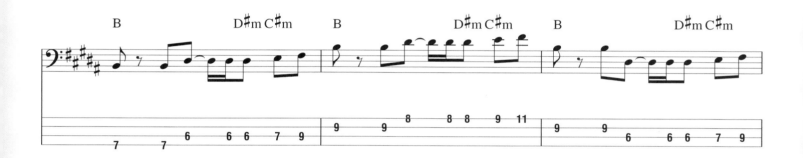

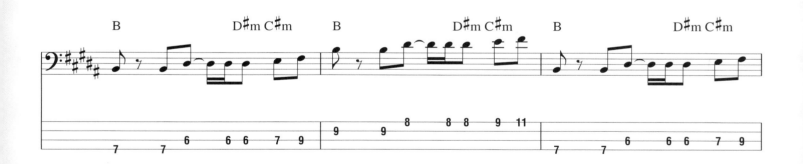

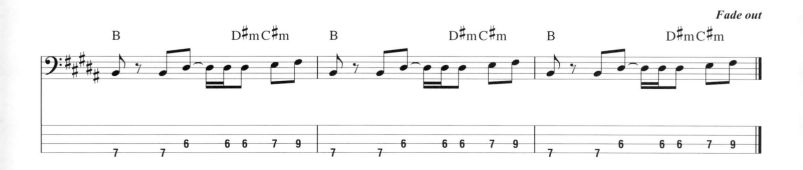

Hold On I'm Comin'

The title of this classic song came about when Isaac Hayes was getting impatient while waiting for David Porter to come out of a bathroom stall so that they could write. Porter yelled back, "Hold on, I'm comin'!" Pay attention to the staccato feel that Duck employed for the verses, in contrast to the legato feel of the chorus.

Sam & Dave
Single, 1966

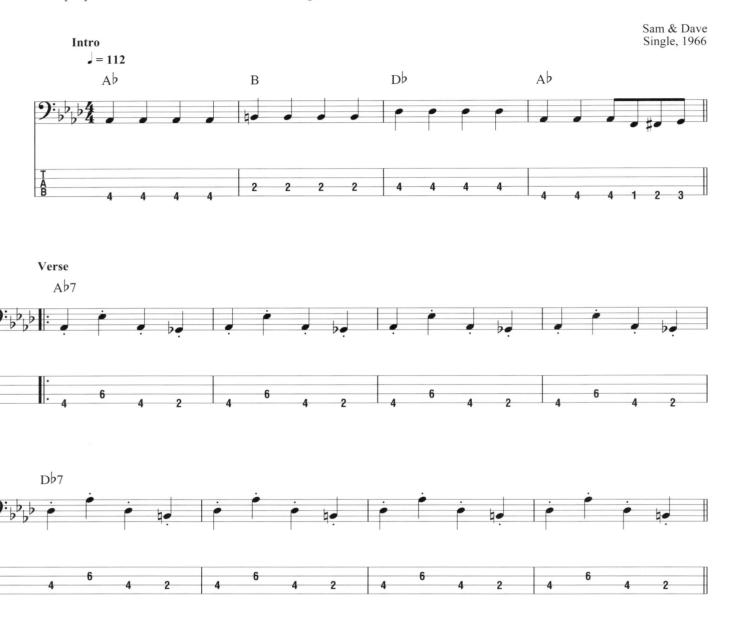

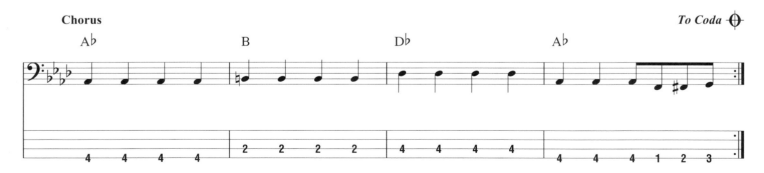

Words and Music by Isaac Hayes and David Porter
Copyright © 1966 IRVING MUSIC, INC. and PRONTO MUSIC
Copyright Renewed
All Rights Reserved   Used by Permission

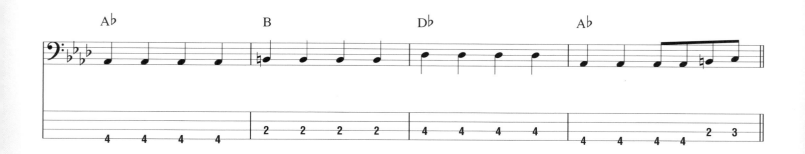

Bridge

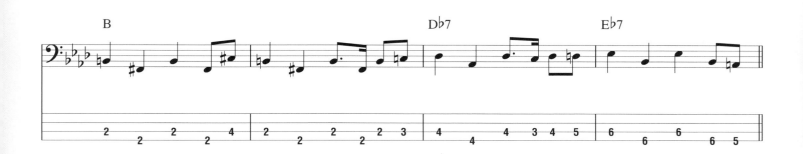

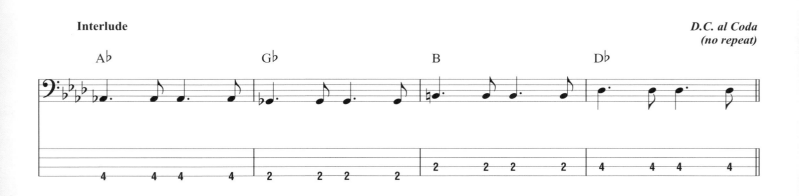

D.C. al Coda
(no repeat)

Interlude

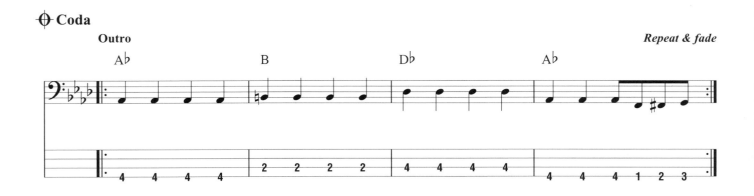

𝄋 **Coda**

Outro   *Repeat & fade*

Ninety-Nine and a Half (Won't Do)

Wilson Pickett
The Exciting Wilson Pickett, 1966

Intro

634-5789

This tune was recorded twice at Stax Records, both within a year or so. Wilson Pickett recorded it in 1966 and Eddie Floyd in 1967. The two versions are in different keys, but the tempo and roadmap are very similar. So it's an interesting study to see how Duck would handle the same song in two different ways. In Pickett's version, he played straight quarter notes in the verse, and on Floyd's, he threw a triplet in on beat 4 of every measure. In both versions, he played eighth notes in the bridge—one with arpeggios and the other with root-fifth movements. In both versions, the root-sixth-fifth pattern is a prevalent factor throughout.

The Wilson Pickett version that accompanies this book features Will Lee on bass.

Wilson Pickett
The Exciting Wilson Pickett, 1966

634-5789

Eddie Floyd
Knock on Wood, 1967

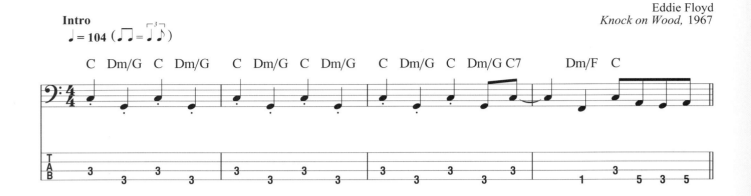

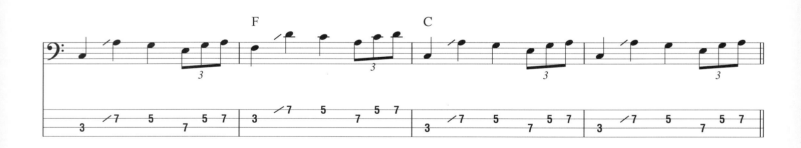

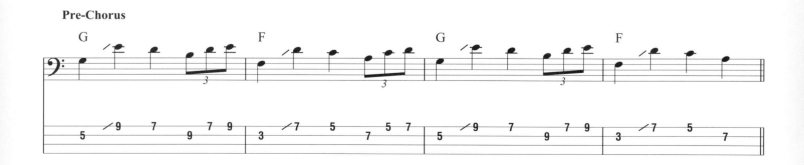

Chorus

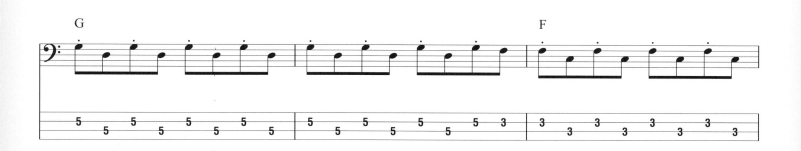

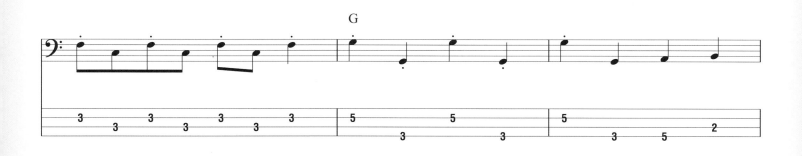

D.S. & fade

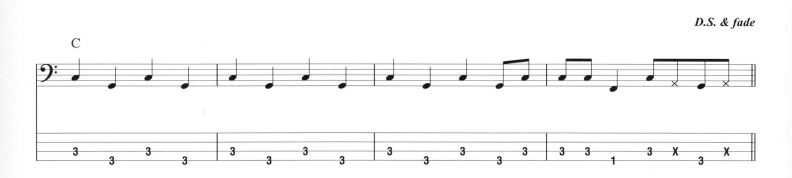

Born Under a Bad Sign

Albert King
Born Under a Bad Sign, 1967

Chorus

Guitar Solo

Bridge

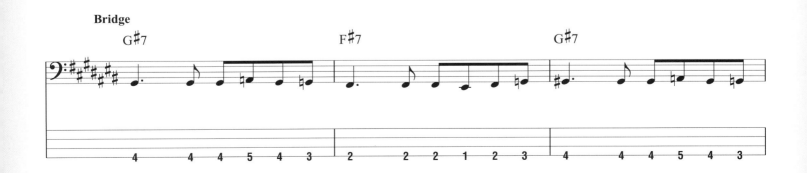

Verse

Chorus

Outro

Repeat & fade

Crosscut Saw

Albert King
Born Under a Bad Sign, 1967

Words and Music by R.G. Ford
Copyright © 1969 IRVING MUSIC, INC.
Copyright Renewed
All Rights Reserved   Used by Permission

Groovin'

Booker T. & the MGs
Hip Hug-Her, 1967

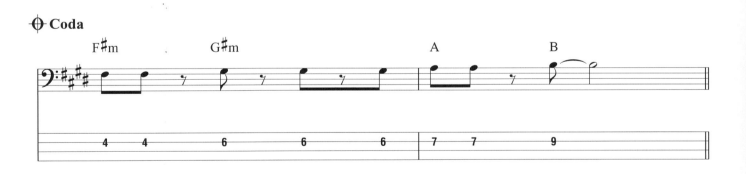

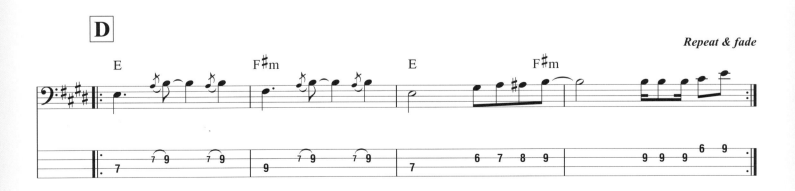

Hip Hug-Her

This song ended up being the band's biggest success since "Green Onions." As Booker said, "That's probably Duck's most aggressive outing, and the sound is just incredible. It's almost breaking up, but it's not. The bass leads the band. The guitar and bass are playing the same thing, which is a sound I've stuck with in my mind. It beefs up the bottom end; it makes a strong statement for a dance record."

This is one of the few instances when Duck had roundwound strings on his bass, rather than flats. Will Lee played the bass part on the track that accompanies this book.

Booker T. & the MGs
Hip Hug-Her, 1967

Wrap It Up

It doesn't seem common for Duck to have dropped his E string down to E-flat, so I asked Steve Cropper. He's pretty sure that Duck never thought about drop tuning. Nonetheless, there is a prominent low E-flat played throughout the tune. Duck seemed to have avoided the E string for most of the song except to play this low E-flat, so it is plausible that he dropped the tuning of just that string to accommodate the verse riff.

Sam & Dave
Single, 1968

Tuning:

E♭-A-D-G

Intro
♩ = 114

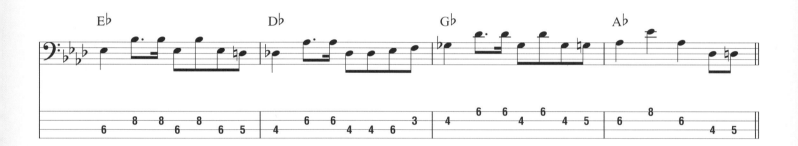

Verse

Chorus

Interlude

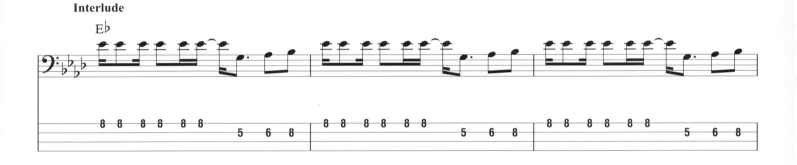

Bridge

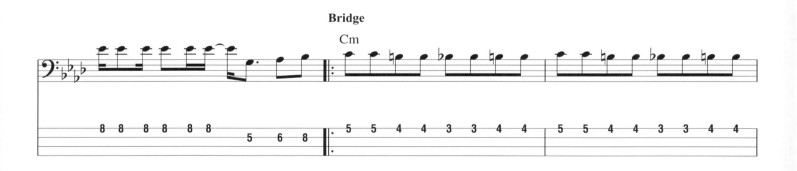

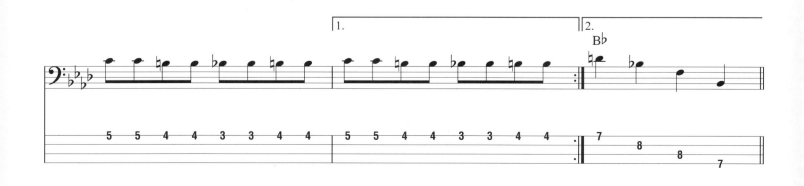

Verse

Chorus

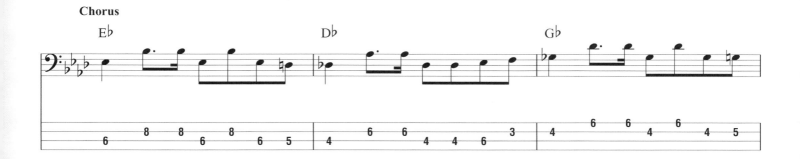

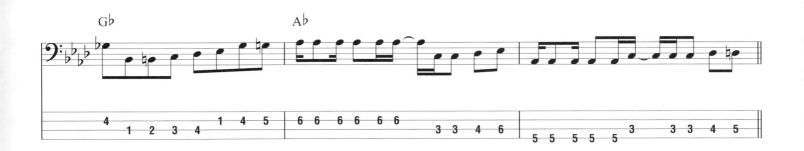

Outro   *Fade out*

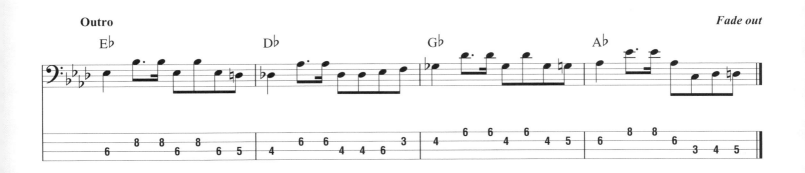

Knock on Wood

An interesting piece of trivia: This song was written by Eddie Floyd and Steve Cropper, but after hearing the demo with Eddie singing on it, Stax decided it wasn't a good fit for Otis. They promoted the demo version with Eddie, and it became a hit. The "knocking" on the snare drum was Al Jackson's idea, and Floyd has said it's what makes the song.

I'd consider this to be the epitome of a Duck Dunn line. It employs syncopation, avoidance of beat 2, root-sixth-fifth movement, a repetitive figure, and that classic Precision bass sound. It's often suggested that the figure was played across three strings (starting the first A note on the 12th fret), but I'm confident that, since Duck tended to slide into the sixth on subsequent live versions of this tune, he would have started the line on the 7th fret.

Eddie Floyd
Knock on Wood, 1967

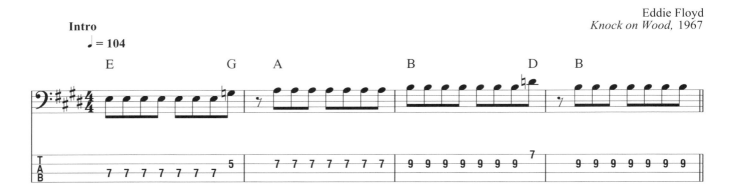

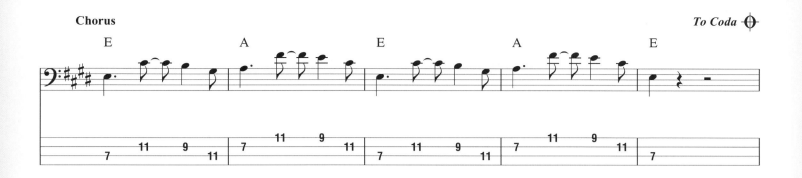

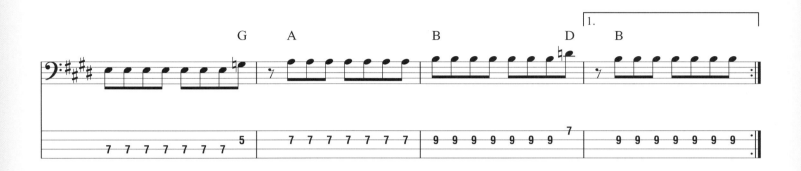

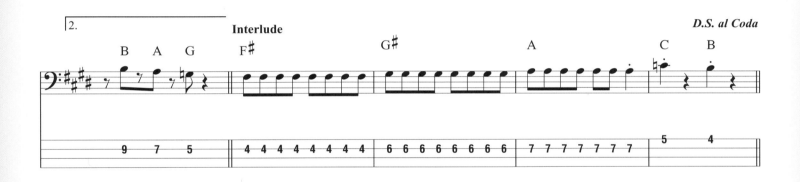

Interlude

⊕ **Coda**

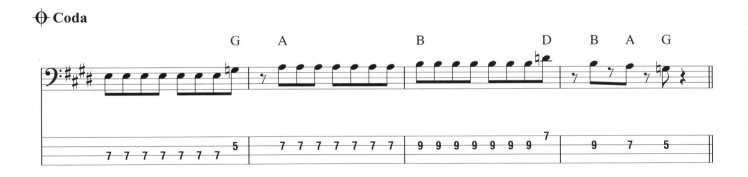

Outro

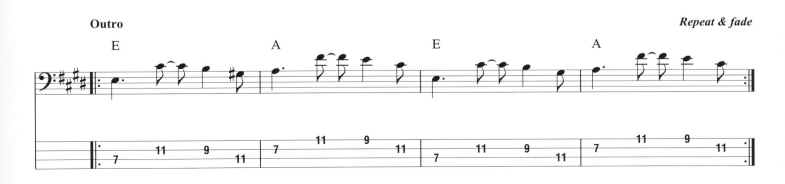

Soul Man

Isaac Hayes was responsible for the bass line on this tune. In an interview in 2009, Duck said "He just, he came up with the bass line. And in particular, it's almost Bo Diddley, you know, that's kind of what it is. But he had that moment, when on the intro and in the middle, that's where he automatic just goes, 'hold the tonic,' then he goes, 'go to the next chord.' And Steve does his guitar fills. And Steve did that with that slide stuff that sounds like Steve's playing; it's done with an old Zippo cigarette lighter."

On the original recording, you can hear Duck "forget" to go to the chorus—he keeps playing the same figure two beats into it, but catches himself by beat 3. This goof is on a song that made it to #2 on the pop charts and shows that even when Duck makes a mistake, he holds the groove.

Jeff Dunn plays bass on the audio track that accompanies this book.

Sam & Dave
Soul Men, 1967

(Sittin' On) The Dock of the Bay

Of course, this was the song that Stax put out soon after Otis died. It was still a work in progress when he passed, but everything had been tracked; it just needed arranging and mixing. Steve Cropper has mentioned that the intro to the song, Duck's root-fifth-fifth feel, was later quoted in the intro to Stevie Wonder's "I Just Called to Say I Love You." While it's considered a ballad, Duck's playing is still heavily groove-oriented rather than a whole-note/half-note feel.

Otis Redding
Single, 1968

Hang 'Em High

Booker T. & the MGs
Soul Limbo, 1968

I Thank You

Sam & Dave
Single, 1968

Intro

♩ = 120

Chorus

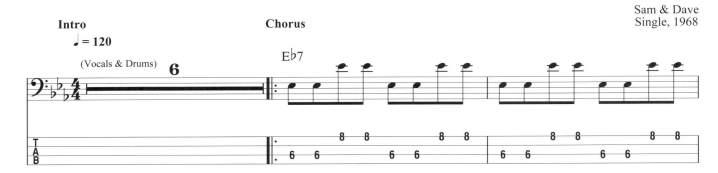

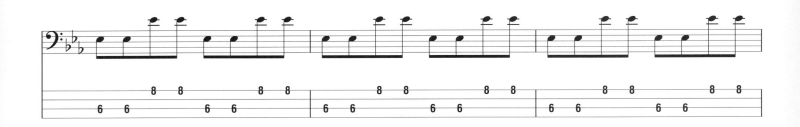

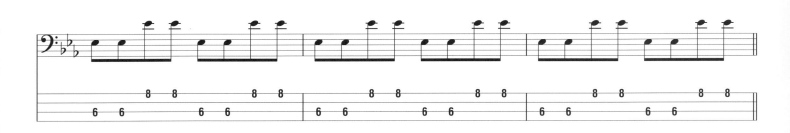

Time Is Tight

Booker wanted to write something that didn't follow a standard four- or eight-bar phrase, and that's where "Time Is Tight" originated. The verse is a 14-measure phrase heavily influenced by "I Can't Turn You Loose." As Booker said, "That just seemed to fit there. Thank God the same guys wrote both of them."

Booker wanted to name the song "Uptight" for the *Up Tight* movie soundtrack he was working on, but since Stevie Wonder already had a song with that title, "Time Is Tight" was what they agreed upon.

Booker T. & the MGs
Up Tight, 1969

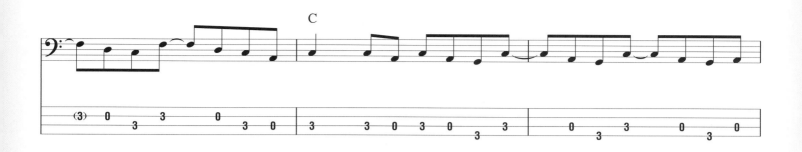

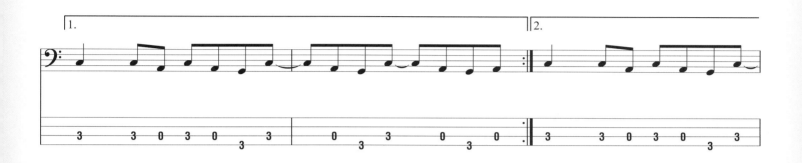

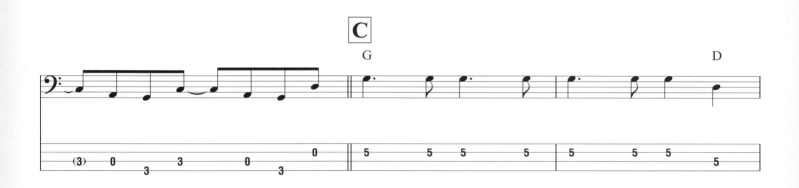

To Next **B**

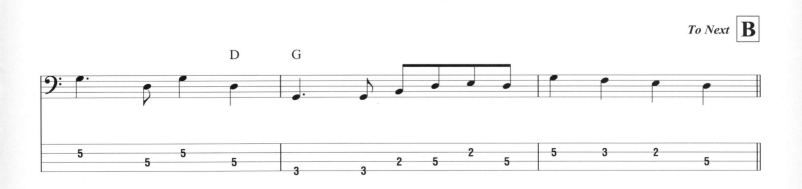

Mean Disposition

The Muddy Waters' album *Fathers and Sons* seems to be one of the sessions that Duck, as well as his family and friends, were especially proud of.

Muddy Waters
Fathers and Sons, 1969

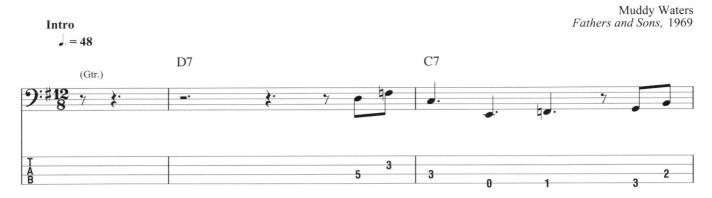

Verse

Verse

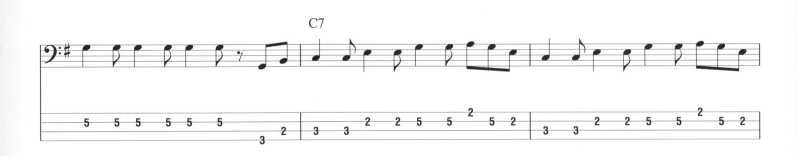

Guitar Solo

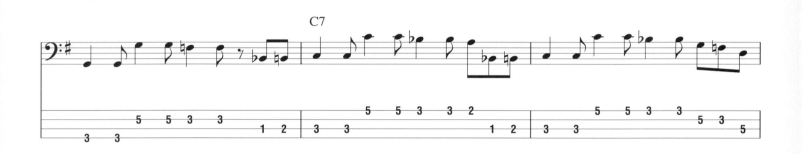

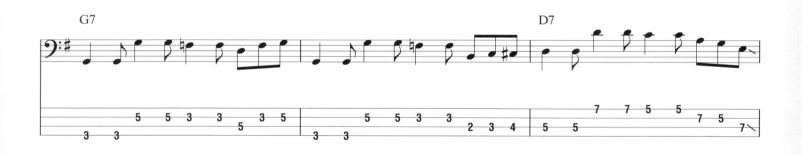

To Piano Solo

Sugar Sweet

Muddy Waters
Fathers and Sons, 1969

Harmonica Solo

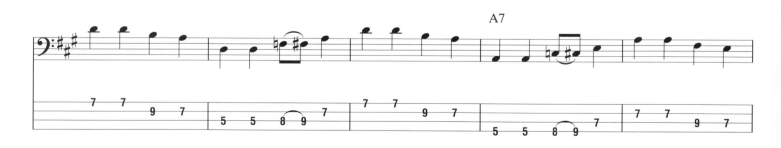

Verse

Walking Through the Park

Muddy Waters
Fathers and Sons, 1969

Intro

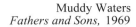

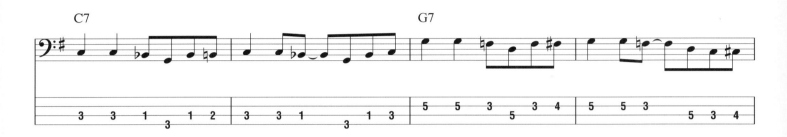

Verse

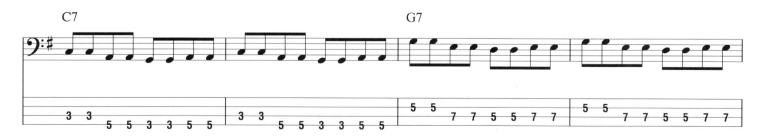

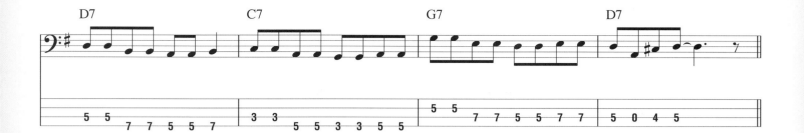

Verse

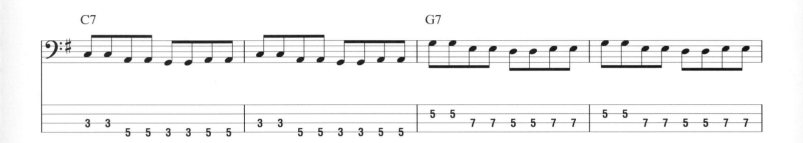

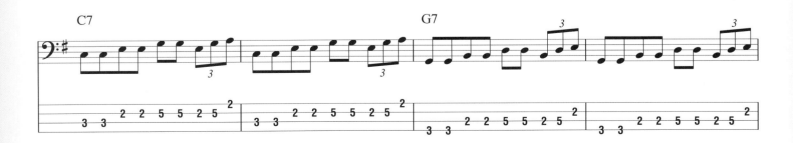

Harmonica Solo

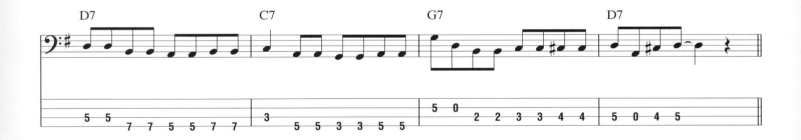

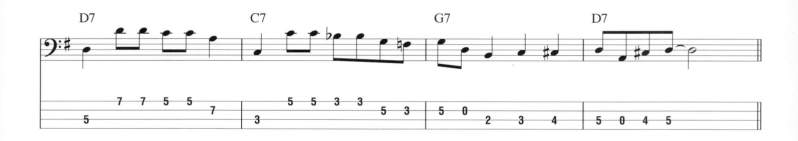

Verse

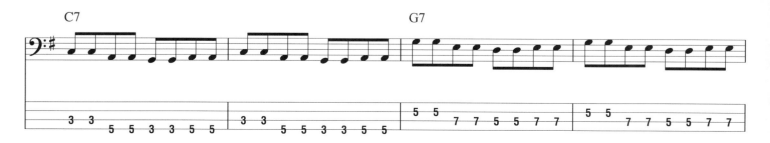

Guitar Solo

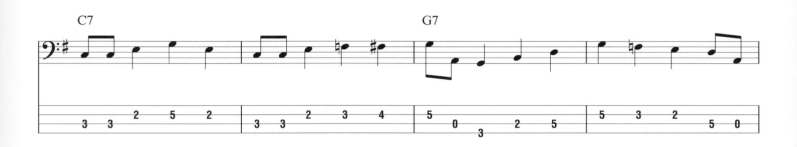

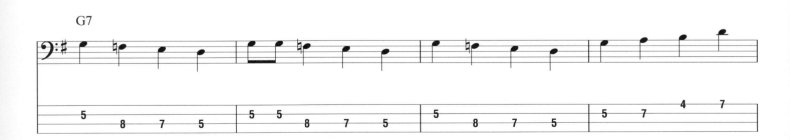

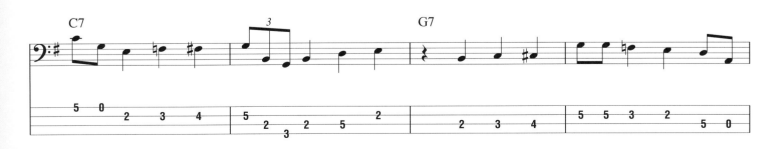

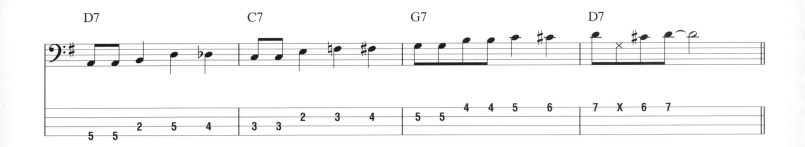

Verse

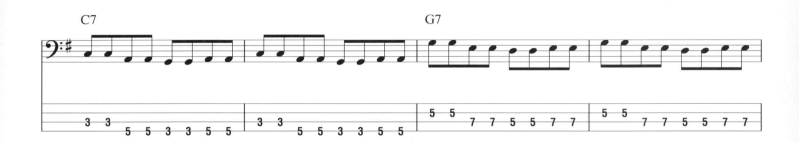

Outro (♫ = ♫)

Play 5 times

Repeat & fade

You Gonna Need Me

Albert King
King of the Blues Guitar, 1969

Ain't No Sunshine

Bill Withers
Single, 1971

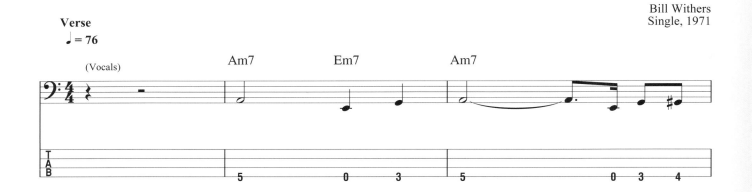

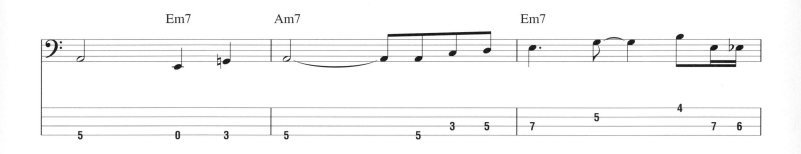

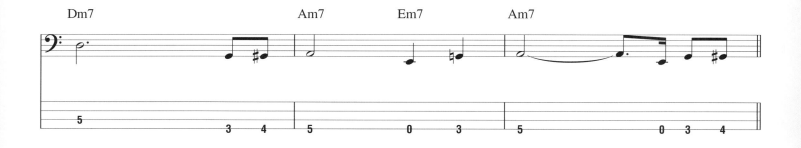

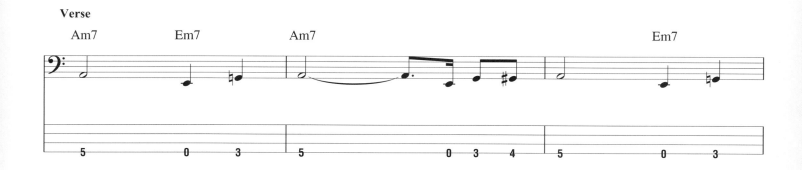

Bridge

Verse

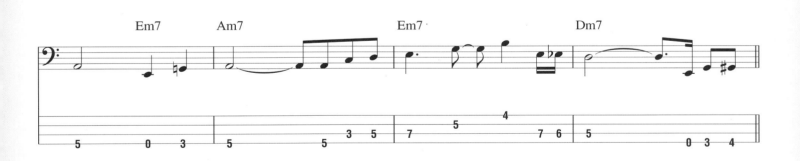

Outro

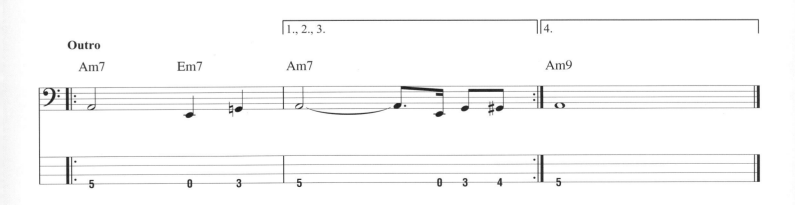

If

Herbie Mann put together an "all-star" cast of musicians for his album *Push Push*, including bassists Jerry Jemmott and Chuck Rainey. Duane Allman played guitar for the whole album. Duck would later admit that this wasn't a type of playing he was comfortable with and eventually figured he should stick to the type of bass playing for which he was known.

Herbie Mann
Push Push, 1971

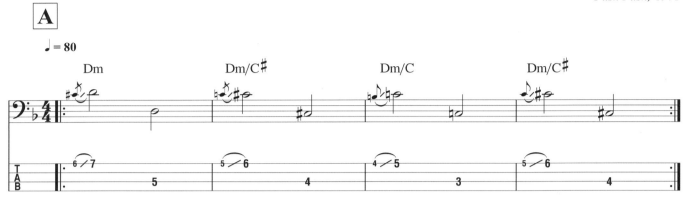

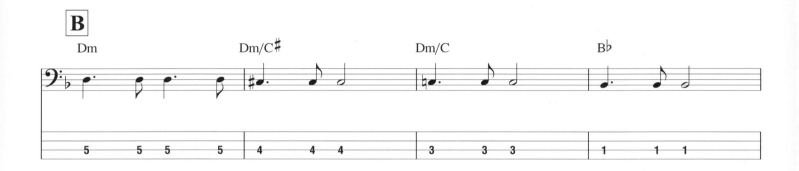

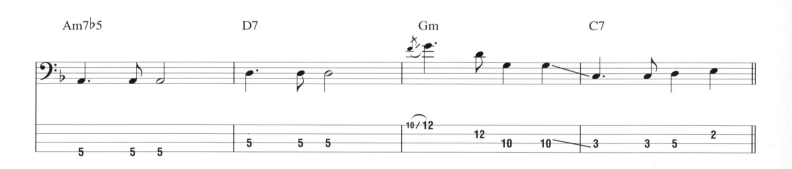

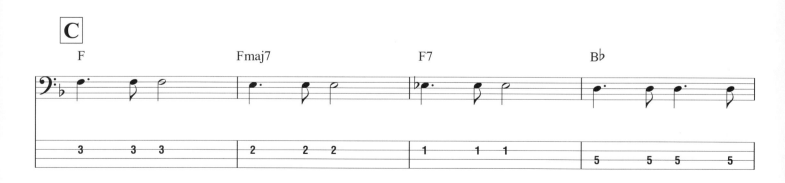

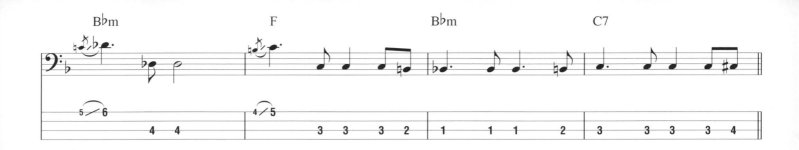

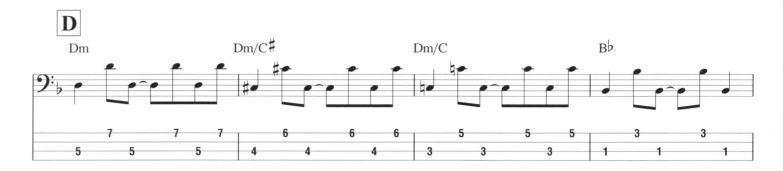

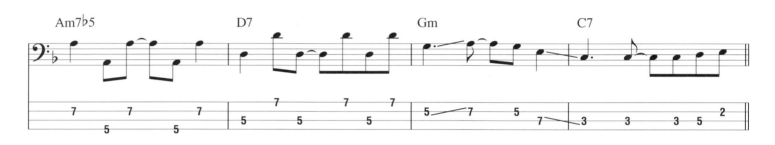

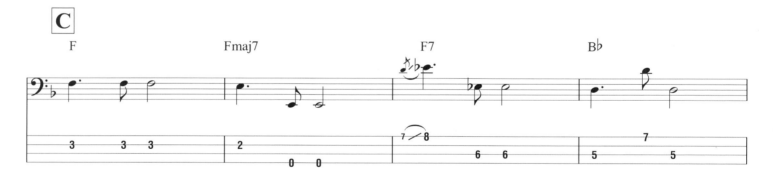

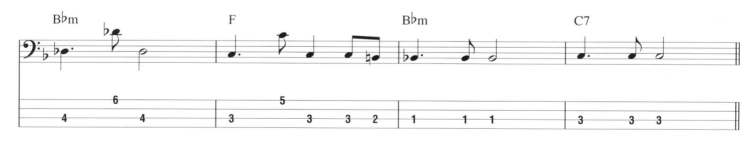

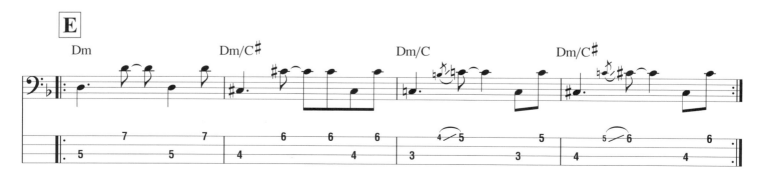

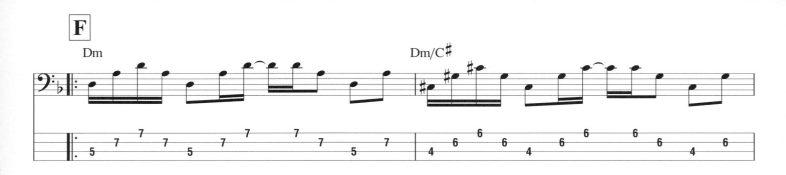

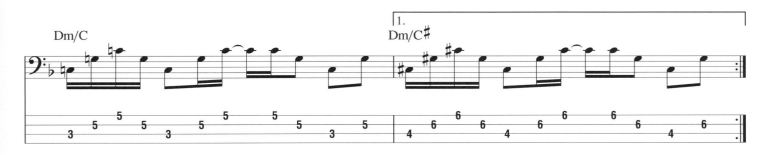

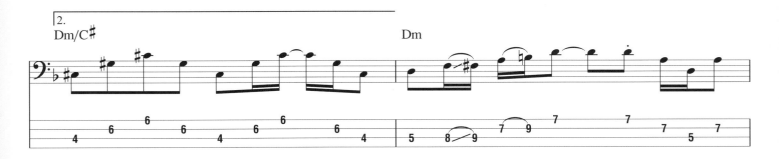

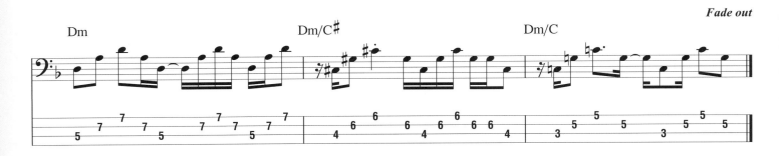

Key to the Highway

This was recorded at Shelter Records in Los Angeles. Don Nix introduced Duck to Leon Russell and Denny Cordell. They started using Duck and eventually introduced him to Tom Petty.

Freddie King
Getting Ready..., 1971

Born to Be a Loser

Although there are reports that Jerry Lee Lewis wasn't easy to work with at this particular session, everyone I've spoken to that was either directly involved or had heard about it through Duck said it was a pleasant experience. This bass line is a personal favorite, simply because it's Duck being Duck, and he gets a little more playful with it.

Jerry Lee Lewis
Southern Roots, 1973

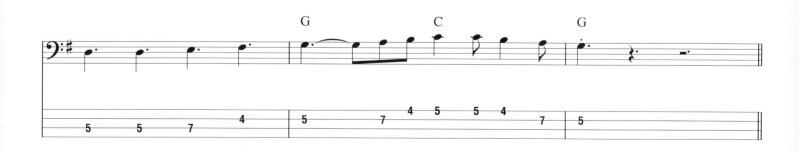

Verse

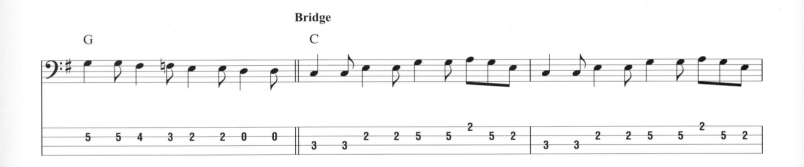

Bridge

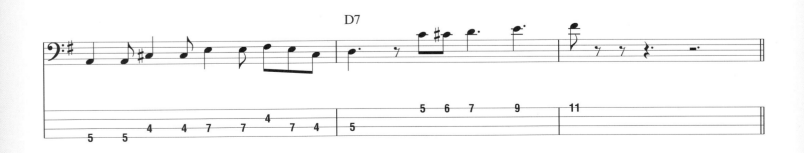

Chorus

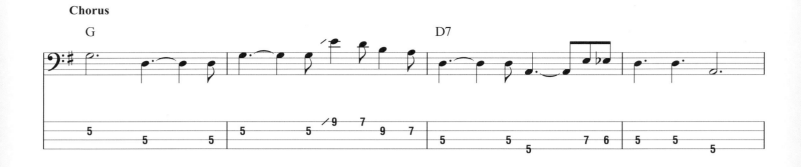

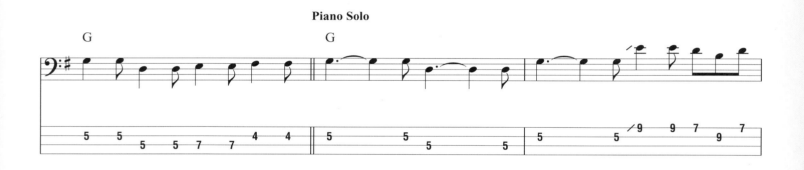

Piano Solo

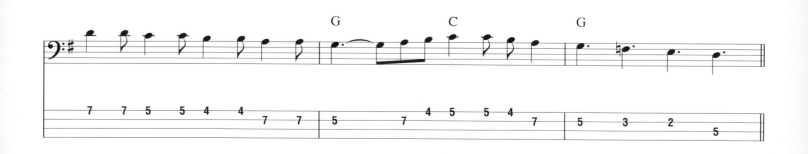

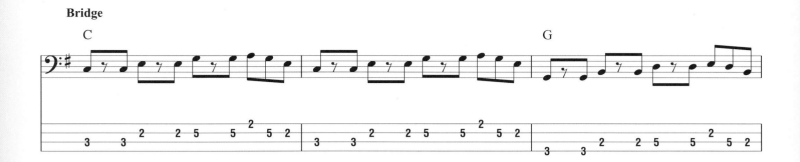

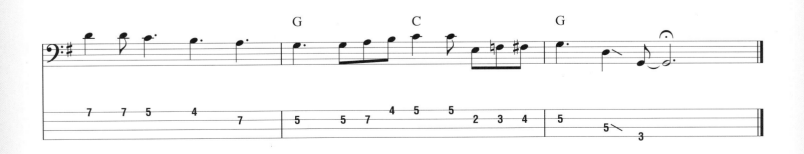

Girl of Mine

Compared to the experience with Jerry Lee, Elvis was a different story. Nothing went the way the Stax musicians expected, and Elvis was followed by a pack of writers who were all trying to get their songs recorded. Although the musicians were expecting to play Stax songs while backing Elvis, they instead were shown demos and told to play the new songs as close to the demo versions as possible. Still, you can hear Duck sneaking in his brand of playing here and there.

Elvis Presley
Raised on Rock, 1973

Woman to Woman

This song was the last hit Stax produced, which staved off their inevitable closure for a little while longer. The intro is a very long vamp, including a soliloquy by Shirley Brown.

The track included with the book repeats only four times, and Duck's "alternate" fill is played the third time through.

Shirley Brown
Single, 1974

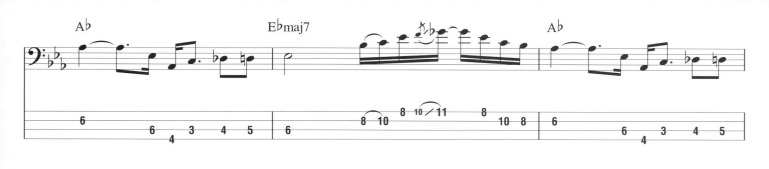

Verse

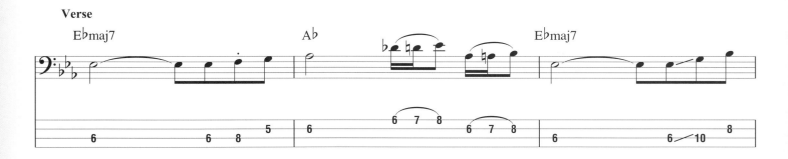

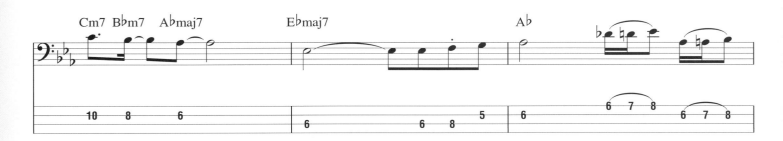

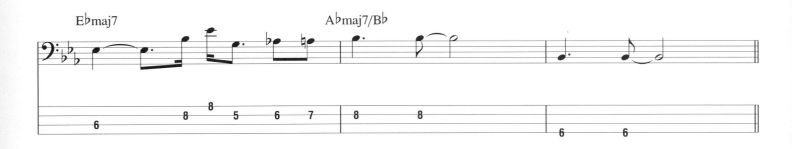

Outro

Repeat & fade

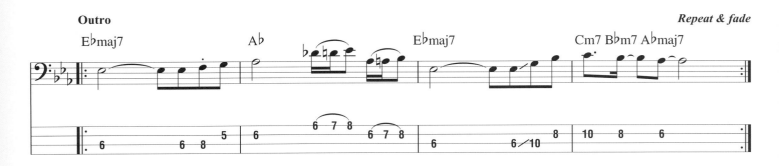

Hometown Blues

Tom Petty once said, "We met in the middle '70s. We were working on our first record at Sound City with Denny Cordell, and Duck and Steve Cropper were working across the hall. We were having a hard time figuring out a bass part, and Denny was like, 'Well, hell, Duck Dunn's across the hall. Let's bring him over and see if he can help.' Duck came in, sat down, listened through the song and then put down the part for us. That's what you hear on 'Hometown Blues' off our first album."

Though Ron Blair played bass for Petty, Duck was still brought in to play on a track here and there. Duck would say, "Tom likes to have me on at least a track per album, because 'Duck brought luck.'"

Tom Petty and the Heartbreakers
Tom Petty and the Heartbreakers, 1976

It's Not the Spotlight

The Manhattan Transfer
Pastiche, 1977

Rubber Biscuit

The Blues Brothers
Briefcase Full of Blues, 1978

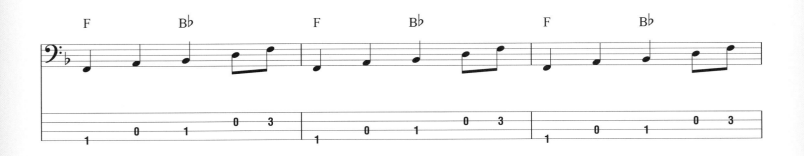

To Next Verse

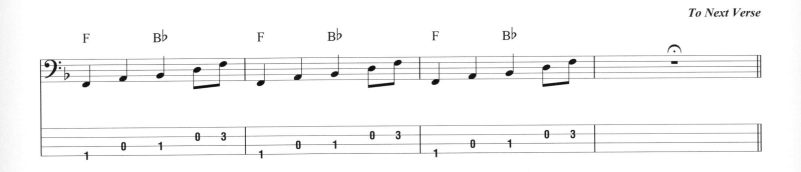

Words and Music by Charles Johnson, Nathaniel Epps, Paul Fulton, Shedrick Lincoln and Samuel Strain
© 1978 EMI LONGITUDE MUSIC
All Rights Reserved   International Copyright Secured   Used by Permission

(I Got Everything I Need) Almost

This song was on the debut album with the Blues Brothers. Duck's line is solid and repetitive, and pedals during the horn break. He also navigates the 2/4 bars flawlessly, making it difficult to notice the time change.

The Blues Brothers
Briefcase Full of Blues, 1978

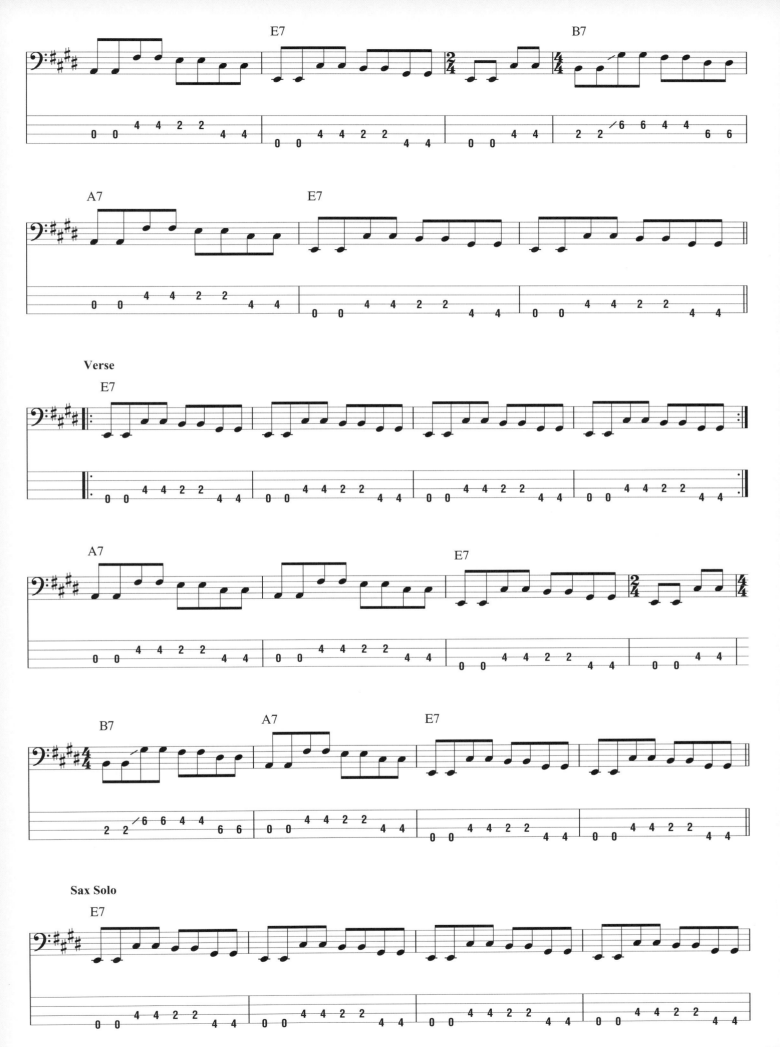

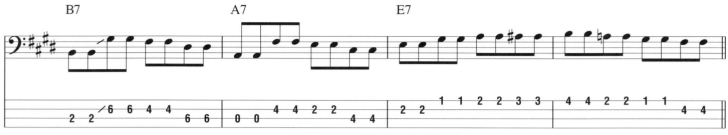

Piano Solo

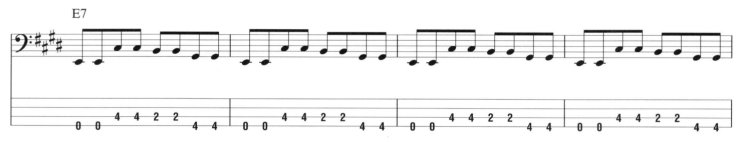

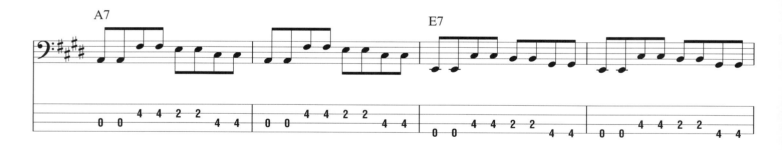

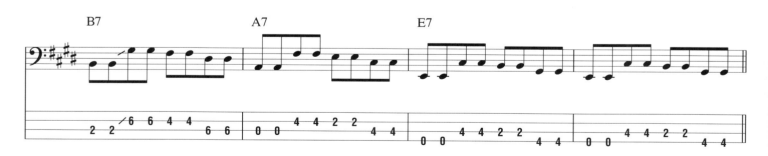

Interlude

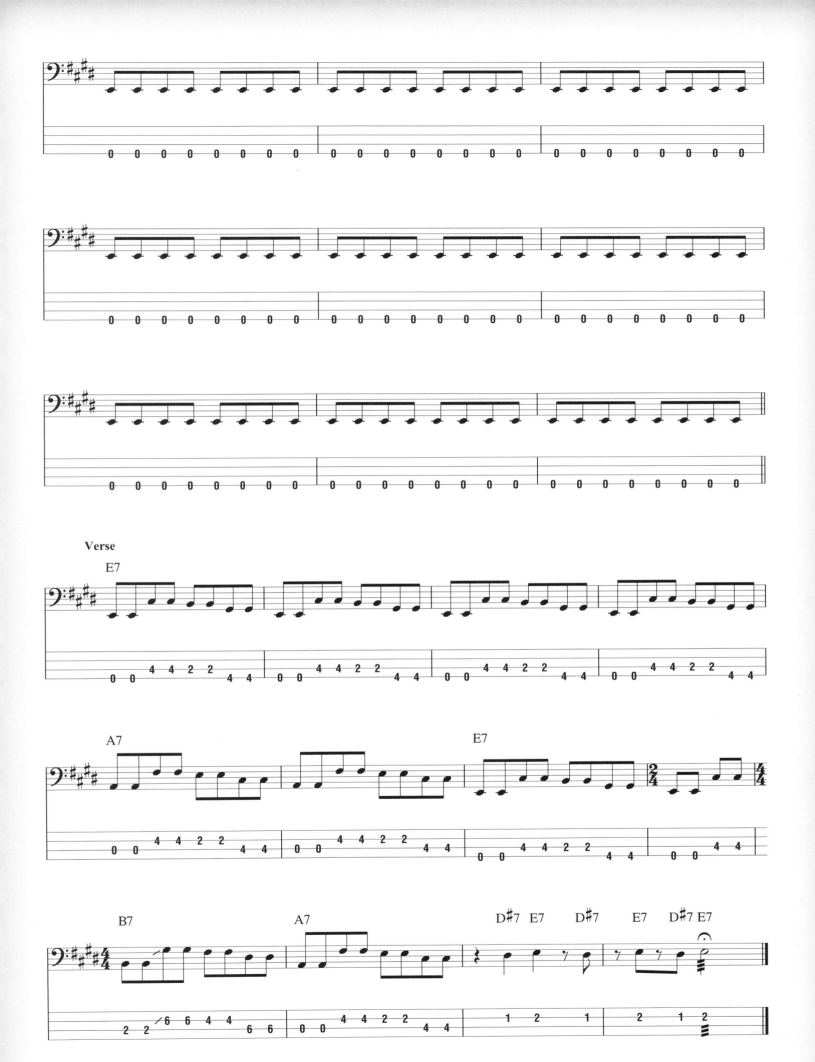

Verse

You Tell Me

Tom Petty and the Heartbreakers
Damn the Torpedoes, 1979

Intro

♩ = 106

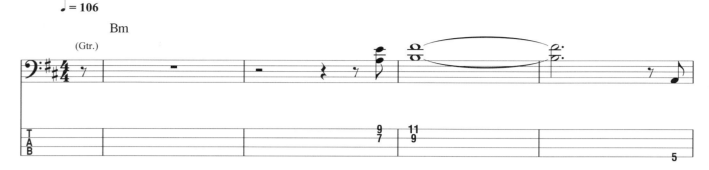

Gimme Some Lovin'

The Blues Brothers
The Blues Brothers soundtrack, 1980

Interlude

Verse

To Coda ⊕

Chorus

D.S. al Coda
(take repeats)

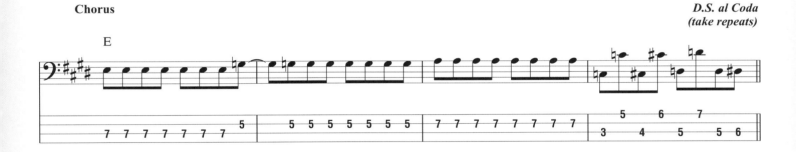

⊕ **Coda**

Chorus

Repeat & fade

Shake a Tail Feather

This tune drives the eighth notes all the way through. It is an interesting departure from Duck's standard "less is more" approach, but does employ the sixth often.

Ray Charles and the Blues Brothers
The Blues Brothers soundtrack, 1980

Verse

♩ = 160

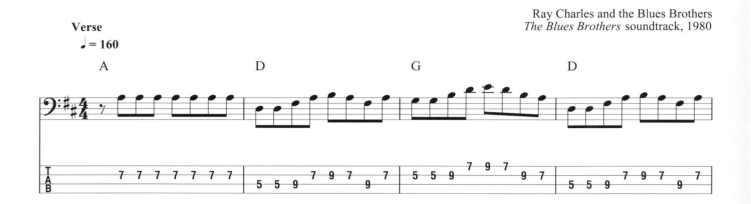

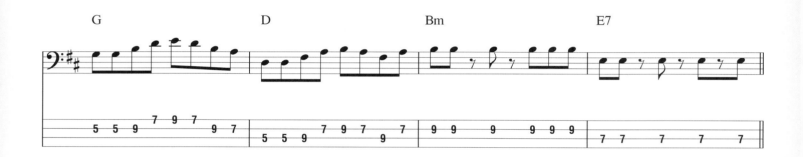

Pre-Chorus

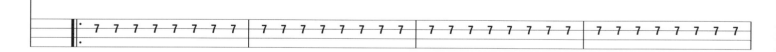

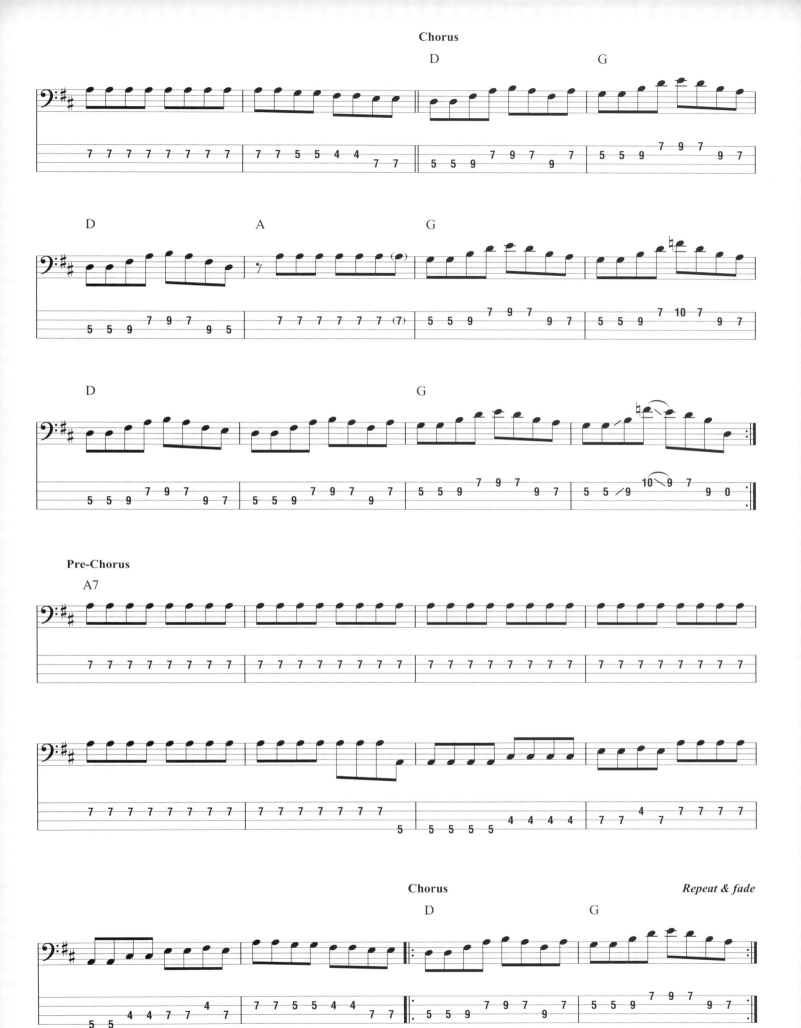

I Ain't Got You

The Blues Brothers
Made in America, 1980

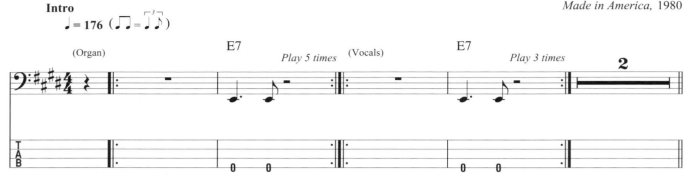

She Caught the Katy

The Blues Brothers
The Blues Brothers soundtrack, 1980

Outro

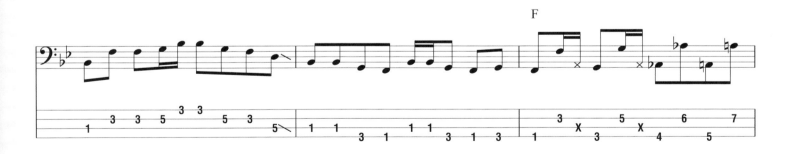

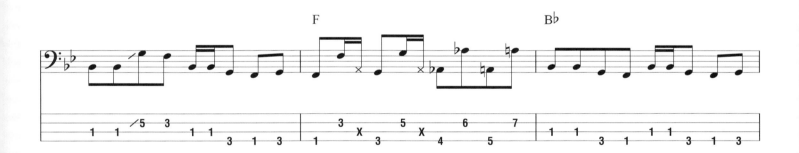

Fade out

Soul Finger/Funky Broadway

While Duck didn't play on the original recording of either of these songs, he especially liked "Funky Broadway." Jeff and June have said that the "Funky Broadway" bass line was regularly the first thing Duck would play when he picked up his bass. It was also his warm-up in the studio.

The Blues Brothers
Made in America, 1980

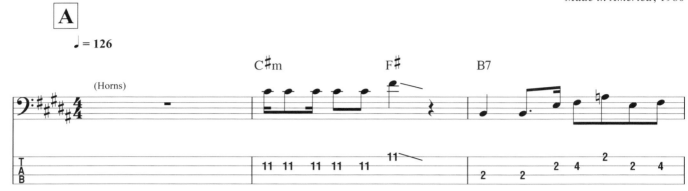

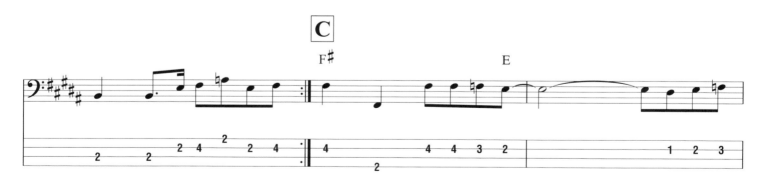

Soul Finger
Words and Music by Ben Cauley, Carl Cunningham, James Alexander, Jimmy King, Phalon Jones and Ronnie Caldwell
Copyright © 1967 IRVING MUSIC, INC.
Copyright Renewed
All Rights Reserved   Used by Permission

Funky Broadway
Words and Music by Arlester Christian
© 1966 (Renewed) Lovolar Music
All Rights Administered by Bike Music c/o The Bicycle Music Company
All Rights Reserved   Used by Permission

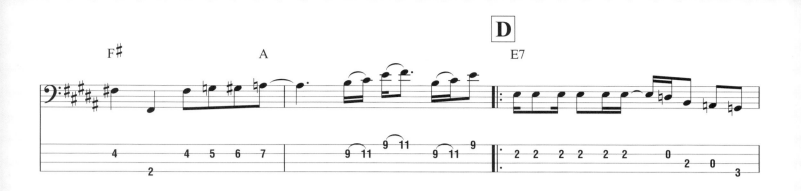

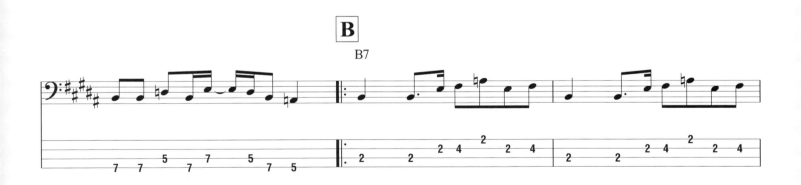

Who's Making Love

The Blues Brothers
Made in America, 1980

Chorus

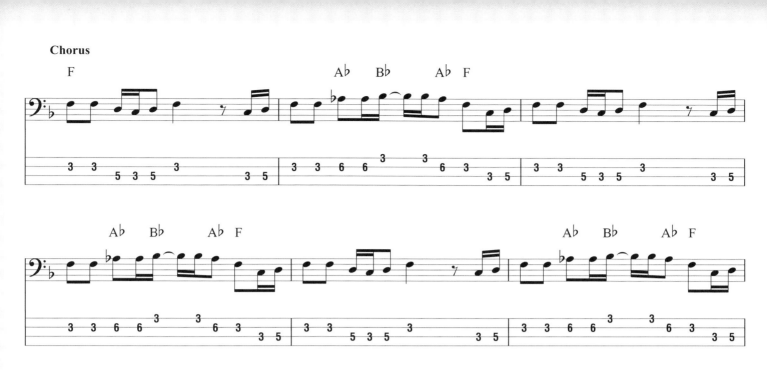

Verse

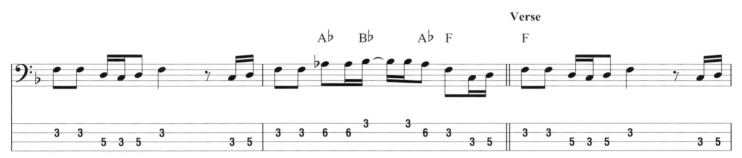

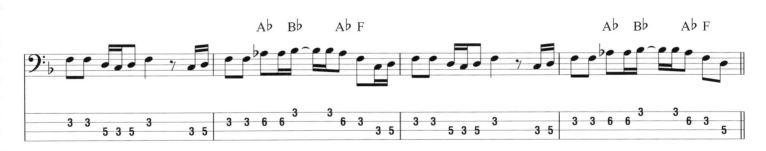

Pre-Chorus

Pre-Chorus

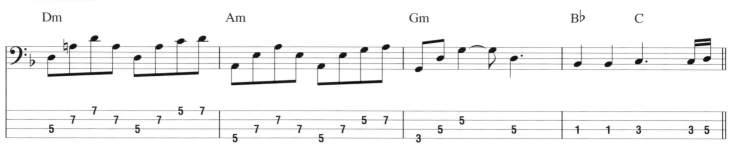

Chorus

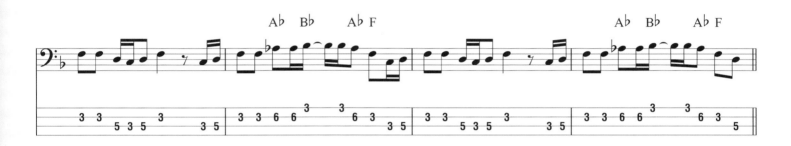

Interlude

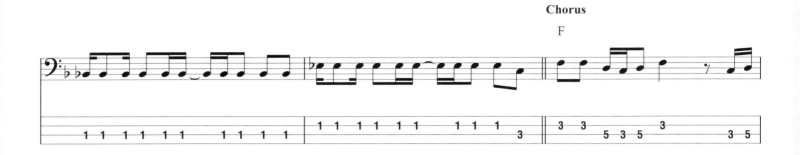

Chorus

F

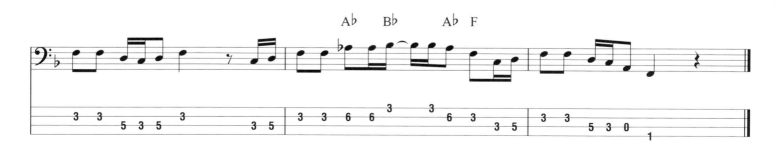

Sweet Home Chicago

This is the tune that inspired me to write this book. It is as masterful a walking bass line as you can get. Towards the end, you can hear Duck experimenting with different "out" things, weaving in and out of the harmony, but never losing the pocket or playing anything that sounds unpleasant.

This is a long recording, but I just couldn't find a way to do it justice by condensing it at all. It has so many important elements a bassist should learn—chromaticism, arpeggiation, pedaling—and yet it still encompasses Duck's style of playing, with many of the measures still revolving around the root-sixth-fifth movement.

The Blues Brothers
The Blues Brothers soundtrack, 1980

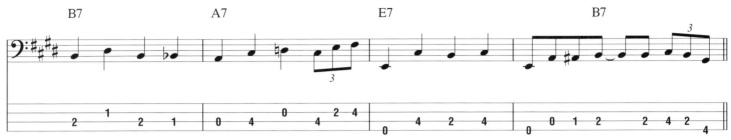

Guitar Solo

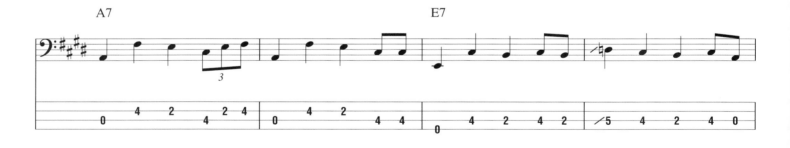

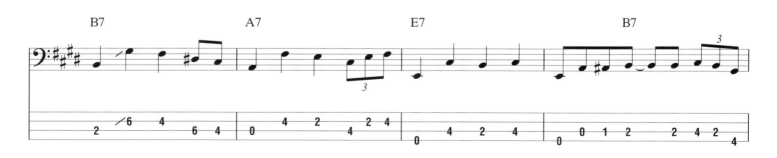

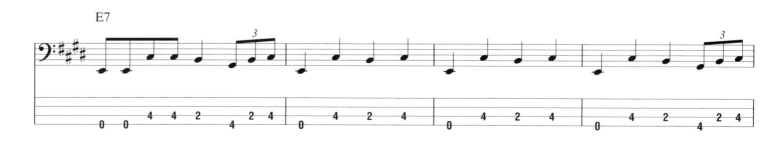

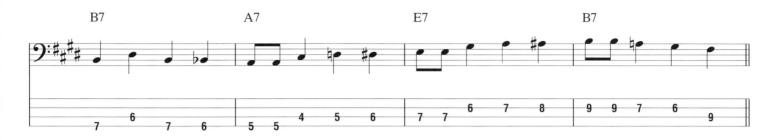

Trombone Solo

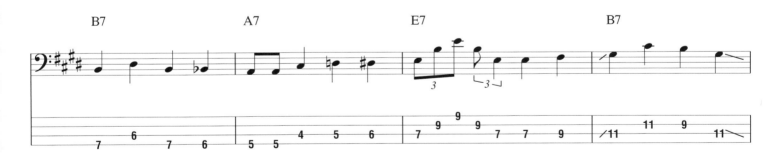

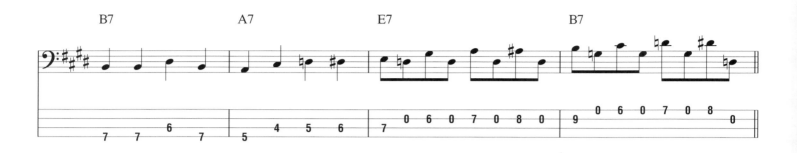

Sax Solo

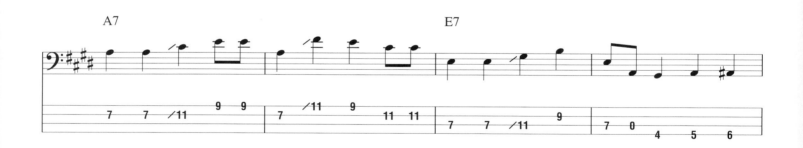

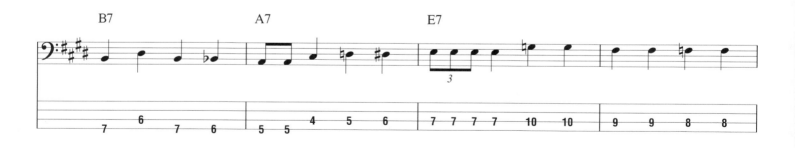

Piano Solo

Outro

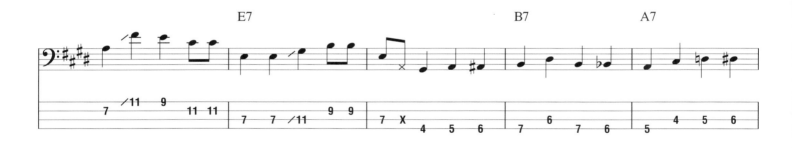

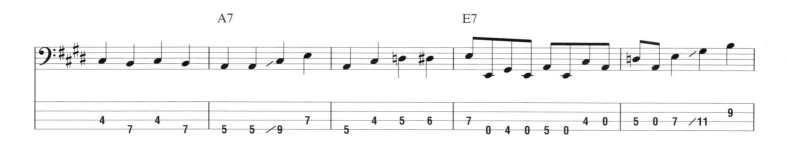

Heart of Mine

Bob Dylan
Shot of Love, 1981

Chorus

To Next Verse

Stop Draggin' My Heart Around

Even though Duck played on this track, it is Ron Blair who is seen in the music video.

Stevie Nicks
Bella Donna, 1981

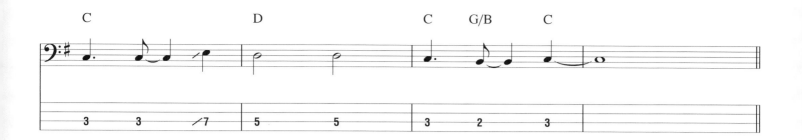

Interlude

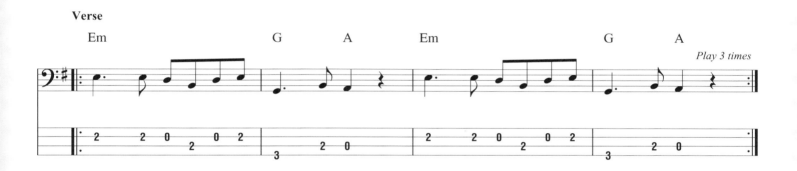

Verse

Play 3 times

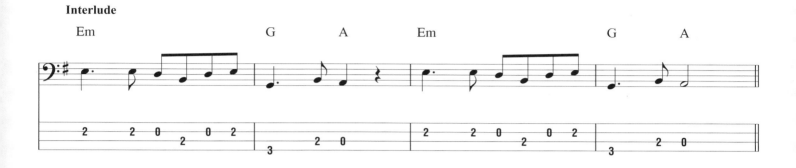

Chorus

To Interlude

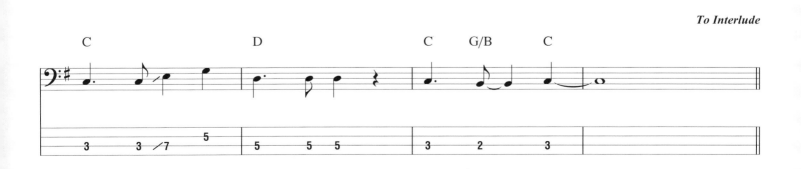

A Woman in Love (It's Not Me)

Tom Petty and the Heartbreakers
Hard Promises, 1981

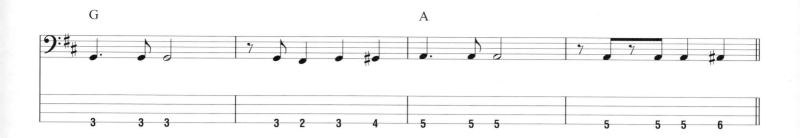

Chorus

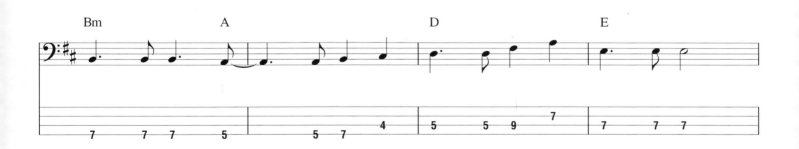

To Next Verse

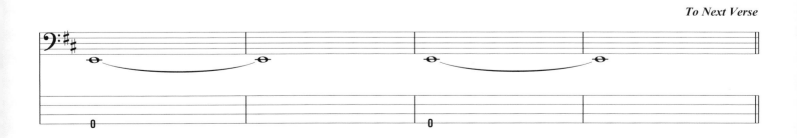

Ain't Going Down

While the note choices throughout this repetitious Clapton tune are almost identical, Duck tends to vary the rhythm to add interest.

Eric Clapton
Money and Cigarettes, 1983

Chorus

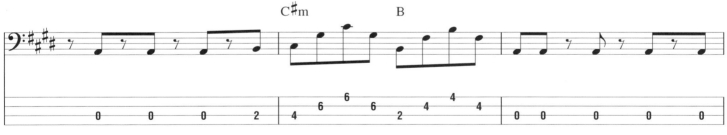

To Next Verse

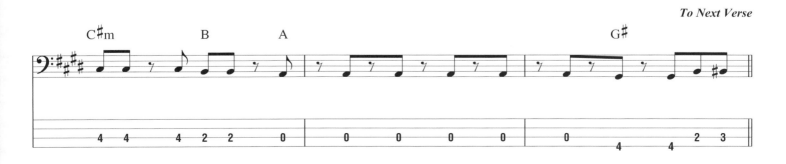

My Barracuda

Jimmy Buffett
Hot Water, 1988

Intro

♩ = 92

Verse

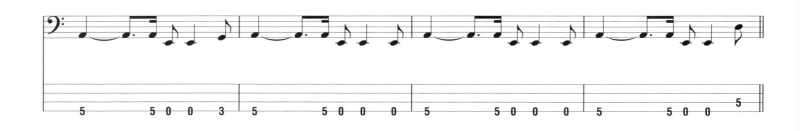

Pre-Chorus

Chorus

Am

Verse

Am

Pre-Chorus

F   C   G   D

Chorus

Am

Bridge

C   Dm   Em   F

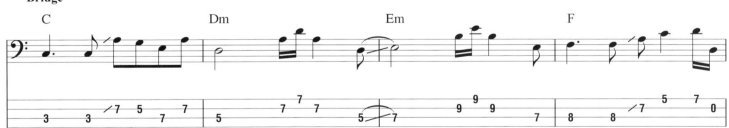

To Guitar Solo

C   Dm   Em   F   E

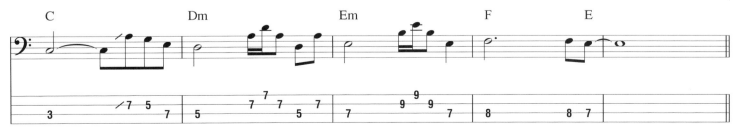

Stand and Be Counted

Crosby, Stills, Nash & Young
Looking Forward, 1999

I Ain't Got Nobody (And Nobody Care for Me)

As far as I can tell, this was the last studio recording Duck played on. It was part of a Jack Black movie in which the jazz standard was a recurring theme. It was interesting to hear this song handled by the MGs, with film director Michel Gondry playing drums in place of Al Jackson. After researching Duck for so long, I would say he probably wasn't a big fan of it. But he gets the job done and lays down a solid line.

Booker T. Jones, Steve Cropper, Donald "Duck" Dunn
Be Kind Rewind soundtrack, 2008

Sources

Books

- *Respect Yourself: Stax Records and the Soul Explosion* (book and movie) – Robert Gordon

- *Soulsville, U.S.A.: The Story of Stax Records* – Rob Bowman

- *Sweet Soul Music: Rhythm and Blues and the Southern Dream of Freedom* – Peter Guralnick

- *Memphis Man: Living High, Laying Low* – Don Nix

- *R&B Bass Masters: The Way They Play* – Ed Friedland

- *A View From the Side: Stories and Perspectives on the Music Business* – Michael Visceglia

Articles/Podcasts

- "Legendary Bassist Donald 'Duck' Dunn Passes" – Ward Meeker, *Vintage Guitar* magazine

- "Duck's Gaggle: The Basses of Donald Dunn" – Ward Meeker, *Vintage Guitar* magazine

- Podcast Encore Special: Donald "Duck" Dunn from March 18, 2015
  (originally aired July 11, 2009) – Michael Shelley, WFMU

- Donald "Duck" Dunn talks to Tim Cashmere at South by Southwest '07 for
  the Stax 50th Anniversary from March 15, 2007 in Austin, Texas

Special Thanks

from the Author

Special thanks to Anton Fig, Brian Johnson, Steve Cropper, Deanie Parker, Don Nix, Dan Aykroyd, Doug Garrison, James Alexander, Larry Nix, Charley Dunn, Steve Potts, Will Lee, Bill Wyman, Dan Lakin, and Bobby Manuel for taking time out of their busy schedules to tell me some great stories.

Thanks to Bob Taylor, Steve Laudicina, Chris Peet, and "Magic" Alex Saenz for doing the hard work to make these recordings go smoothly.

An especially big thanks to Jeff and June Dunn for keeping me on track, offering any help they could, and creating a very smooth working atmosphere, even when I was slacking off. Also thanks to everyone who spoke to Jeff Dunn about the book that I did not have the pleasure to talk to.

To everyone who expressed excitement and encouragement about this project.

And thanks to my parents, for without this sentence, I wouldn't hear the end of it.

from the Duck Dunn Family

The Dunn relatives and family, the Chaillet relatives and family, Dan Aykroyd and family, Steve Cropper and family, Booker T. Jones and family, Al Jackson Jr. and family, Brian and Brenda Johnson, Will Lee, Nick Rosaci, Jeff Schroedl, Kurt Plahna and the Hal Leonard family, Don Nix, Steve Potts, Anton Fig, Bill Wyman, Jim Spake, Bobby Manuel, Neil Young, Eric Clapton, Tom Petty, John and Judy Belushi, Chris Peet, Steve Laudicina, Bob Taylor, Alex Saenz and Legacy Studios, Mike Strick, Leo Binetti, Manny Cruz, David Jacobs, David Staten, Deanie Parker, Andy Tennille, Dan Lakin, Ted Kornblum, Fender Basses, Ampeg Amplifiers, Ward Meeker and the *Vintage Guitar* magazine family, Mike Leahy, Hiromi Mitsuka and family, Tony Joe White and family, Jim Stewart and family, Estelle Axton and family, Dolores Cain and family, Curtis Welch and family, Harold Boone, Al Young, Roxanne Vlcek, and Rick Vrtis.

...and any folks not mentioned by name above who touched our lives during Duck's journey and beyond.

www.facebook.com/DuckDunnRemembered

www.duckdunnremembered.com

www.duckdunn.com

Song Index

*Includes audio track

Bass Notation Legend

Bass music can be notated two different ways: on a *musical staff,* and in *tablature.*

Notes:

THE MUSICAL STAFF shows pitches and rhythms and is divided by bar lines into measures. Pitches are named after the first seven letters of the alphabet.

TABLATURE graphically represents the bass fingerboard. Each horizontal line represents a string, and each number represents a fret.

Strings:

3rd string, open   2nd string, 2nd fret   1st & 2nd strings open, played together

HAMMER-ON: Strike the first (lower) note with one finger, then sound the higher note (on the same string) with another finger by fretting it without picking.

PULL-OFF: Place both fingers on the notes to be sounded. Strike the first note and without picking, pull the finger off to sound the second (lower) note.

LEGATO SLIDE: Strike the first note and then slide the same fret-hand finger up or down to the second note. The second note is not struck.

SHIFT SLIDE: Same as legato slide, except the second note is struck.

TRILL: Very rapidly alternate between the notes indicated by continuously hammering on and pulling off.

TREMOLO PICKING: The note is picked as rapidly and continuously as possible.

VIBRATO: The string is vibrated by rapidly bending and releasing the note with the fretting hand.

SHAKE: Using one finger, rapidly alternate between two notes on one string by sliding either a half-step above or below.

NATURAL HARMONIC: Strike the note while the fret hand lightly touches the string directly over the fret indicated.

MUFFLED STRINGS: A percussive sound is produced by laying the fret hand across the string(s) without depressing them and striking them with the pick hand.
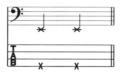

BEND: Strike the note and bend up the interval shown.

BEND AND RELEASE: Strike the note and bend up as indicated, then release back to the original note. Only the first note is struck.
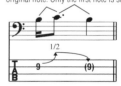

RIGHT-HAND TAP: Hammer ("tap") the fret indicated with the "pick-hand" index or middle finger and pull off to the note fretted by the fret hand.

LEFT-HAND TAP: Hammer ("tap") the fret indicated with the "fret-hand" index or middle finger.

SLAP: Strike ("slap") string with right-hand thumb.

POP: Snap ("pop") string with right-hand index or middle finger.

Additional Musical Definitions

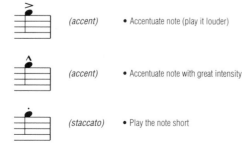

(accent)   • Accentuate note (play it louder)

(accent)   • Accentuate note with great intensity

(staccato)   • Play the note short

D.S. al Coda   • Go back to the sign (𝄋), then play until the measure marked *"To Coda"*, then skip to the section labelled *"Coda."*

Fill   • Label used to identify a brief pattern which is to be inserted into the arrangement.

• Repeat measures between signs.

• When a repeated section has different endings, play the first ending only the first time and the second ending only the second time.